A Guide To Hospital Calling

For Deacons, Elders, and Other Laypersons

Dennis E. Saylor

Baker Book House
Grand Rapids, Michigan 49506

To our sons,

Dennis Alan

and

Douglas Brian

Copyright 1983 by
Baker Book House Company

ISBN: 0-8010-8233-1

First printing, August 1983
Second printing, August 1984

Printed in the United States of America

Contents

Foreword   7

Preface   9

PART ONE   Principles of Hospital Visitation

1   The Purposes of Visiting   13

2   Some Basic Principles   18

3   Religion and Health: *A Holistic Approach*   23

4   Moral Dilemmas in Medicine   29

5   The Hospital Environment   33

6   Relationships with the Hospital Staff   38

PART TWO   General Patient Visitation

7   Meeting the Unexpected   45

8   The Terminal Patient   51

9   The Surgical Patient   60

10   The Medical Patient   66

PART THREE   Specific Patient Visitation

11   The Cancer Patient   73

12   The Orthopedic Patient   80

13   The Geriatric Patient   87

14   The Pediatric Patient   93

15   The Renal Patient   99

16   The Cardiac Patient   105

     Appendixes

A   A Glossary of Common Medical Terms   113

B   Suggested Scripture Readings and Prayers   115

C   Case Studies   118

Foreword

The helping professions and the wider religious community will be excited by this distinctive work. The author has become one of the leading voices today in guiding those who visit hospitals and health-care centers. Dennis Saylor has combined the intellectual understanding of methods of visiting people with the practical dynamic of how this works best for everyone—the patient, the professionals, and the concerned visitor. I cannot overestimate the value of this fine book, for in its contents the reader will discover not only a guide to hospital calling but a guide to life itself.

David Poling

Preface

An avowed purpose of this volume is to present the church visitor with technically correct information in nontechnical language. To achieve this goal I have enlisted the aid of several members of the medical and nursing staff of Presbyterian Hospital (Albuquerque). I acknowledge especially the assistance of Dale Erickson, M.D., Richard Lueker, M.D., and Carol Pierce, R.N., who have been particularly helpful in reading the manuscript and giving pertinent suggestions. I also wish to thank the administrators of Presbyterian Hospital, LaVand Syverson and Robert Shafer, for their encouragement and support, and Marilyn Mercurio, who ably typed the several drafts of the manuscript.

A portion of chapter 2 is adapted from . . . *And You Visited Me* (Morse, 1979); chapters 14 and 15 are adapted from workshop papers I presented at the annual conventions of the College of Chaplains (published in the *Bulletin*, vol. 45, no. 3 [1981]: 50-54, and vol. 46, no. 3 [1982]: 97-101).

PART ONE

Principles
of Hospital Visitation

1

The Purposes of Visiting

Hospitalization presents a unique opportunity for ministry by the local church. Perhaps at no other time in a person's life are spiritual issues confronted so directly. The meaning and purpose of life, death, and suffering are all brought into one's thinking. The person who is hospitalized will often question God's love and protective care more than at any other time.

One cannot read the New Testament and fail to be impressed by the emphasis placed on the healing ministry of Christ and the apostles. Our Lord's evident compassion for the sick is a major theme of the Gospels. Many of His miracles involve healing of the body in connection with healing of the soul.

Jesus' Healing

A brief examination of Christ's healing ministry brings out two special points of interest. First, physical and spiritual healing were inseparable. Second, healing was both mediate and immediate, that is, both with and without a medium or agent. It is important that these characteristics be examined more closely.

Sin and Sickness

Throughout the Gospels Christ treats both bodily and spiritual problems—sickness and sin. For example, to the paralytic let down through the roof He says, "Man, your sins are forgiven you" (Luke 5:20). He refers to the woman who is unable to walk erect as being bound by Satan (Luke 13:16). At the same time He scrupulously avoids seeing a cause-and-effect relationship between sin and particular sicknesses. Consider the Lord's words to the disciples, who assumed that either the blind man or his parents were responsible for the man's blindness. Jesus instructs His disciples, "It was not that this man sinned, or his parents, but that the works of God might be made manifest in him" (John 9:3).

What do the Scriptures teach, then, regarding the relationship between man's sin and sickness? They teach that death came by man's sin (Rom. 5:12). As a cause of death, illness is one of the consequences of sin. Since illness and injury can lead to death, they are sin-related.

We humans are sinners not only as a result of the sin of Adam which is imputed to us and puts us in need of God's redemptive act in Christ. We are also sinners because we ourselves commit willful, sinful acts. Some of those acts can lead to physical illness or injury. Deliberate self-abuse in the form of excessive indulgence in tobacco or alcohol seems to be related to lung cancer and cirrhosis of the liver respectively.

The church visitor needs to be especially sensitive in dealing with this type of illness, for the patient may feel that God is singling him out for abusing his body. This may lead to bitterness and lack of acceptance of his condition. Or the patient may feel that since he is guilty of not taking care of himself, he does not deserve to get well. Such attitudes are hindrances to recovery. If they are present the task of the church visitor is twofold: to assure the patient of God's unfailing love in time of illness, and to assure the patient that he is not going to be critical of the patient's lifestyle.

Mediate and Immediate Healing

The second characteristic of Christ's healing ministry is that His healing was both mediate and immediate. That is, He healed some sufferers by using some type of medium, whereas other healings were wrought directly, without the use of any medium or agent.

An example of mediate healing is the healing of the blind man (John 9). According to the Gospel writer, Jesus made clay from dust and spittle and applied it to the man's eyes. He then instructed the man to wash it off in the pool of Siloam (9:6-7). In other instances Christ instructed the ill to go and show themselves to the priest (for example, the ten lepers—Luke 17:14). When He healed Peter's mother-in-law, He took her by the hand and lifted her up (Mark 1:29-31). The woman with the issue of blood was healed when she touched the fringe of Jesus' garment (Luke 8:43-48).

Immediate healing, on the other hand, is a direct healing using no means or instruments. Many of our Lord's miracles of healing were of this type. The nobleman's son, for example, recovered without even a touch from Jesus (John 4:46-54). This miracle also shows healing in response to the plea of another, in this case the boy's father.

What is important here is to recognize that God may heal with or without some type of agency. In our day most of God's healing is done mediately, using physicians and medicines. However, God's healing grace is not limited, for He still accomplishes healing without human means or agents. It is necessary to bear in mind that both types are examples of divine healing.

For the church visitor the implications are clear. It is fitting and appropriate to pray for God's help for those engaged in the healing arts. At the same time it must be borne in mind that all healing is miraculous and comes from God alone. The church visitor should help the hospitalized patient maintain that balance between trust in those whom God uses to dispense His healing grace and trust in God alone as the giver of that grace.

Apostolic Tradition

In the Gospels, Christ sent out not only the twelve disciples, but the seventy as well (Matt. 10:1-42; Luke 10:1-12). Because He sent them to minister to the sick in His name, Christians from the early church on have clearly understood that they also have a mandate to visit the sick.

That the apostles continued to be engaged in a healing ministry as an adjunct to their preaching is demonstrated in the Book of Acts. The healing of the lame man by Peter and John at the temple gate is but one example (Acts 3:1-10). Paul in his ministry healed the lame man at Lystra (Acts 14:8-10), and handkerchiefs and aprons which had touched Paul's body were used to heal the sick (Acts 19:11-12). We see, then, the same pattern of healing— mediate and immediate—here as well. Further, the apostle Luke was referred to as the "beloved physician" (Col. 4:14).

Down through the succeeding centuries of church history, many have claimed the "gift of healing" (1 Cor. 12:9). Although it is one of the spiritual gifts which are given for the building up of the church, healing has often been ignored by the church. Too often it has abandoned the gift of healing in favor of physical medicine alone.

In apostolic times, however, healing was a significant ministry of the local church. The apostle James gives a brief account of the healing function of a local congregation: "Is any among you sick? Let him call for the elders of the church, and let them pray over him, anointing him with oil in the name of the Lord; and the prayer of faith will save the sick man, and the Lord will raise him up; and if he has committed sins, he will be forgiven" (James 5:14–15).

These verses indicate that healing is a valid ministry of the church. Anointing is the medium advised, but of course the prayer of faith is the essential element of healing. Sin is also dealt with. These verses describe what could well serve as a model for the contemporary church visitor. In fact, James' formulation might be summarized thus:

1. Be present as a representative of the local church.
2. Be prayerful and believe in the healing power of God.
3. Be prepared to use or support whatever medium or agency is significant to the patient.
4. Be purposeful in extending God's love and forgiveness of sin.

Often the modern hospital is sponsored by or affiliated with the church in some way. The local church should not, however, be content with that effort alone. Nor should deacons, elders, and lay ministers, as well as ordained clergy, discount or minimize their role in the healing process or their place in the hospital setting.

The church visitor can and should have a very positive impact on the hospitalized patient. The value of that therapeutic relationship must never be underestimated by anyone. In order to maximize this healing contact the chapters following will endeavor to give helpful guidelines and techniques to that end.

In summary, the local church ministry should be involved in the visiting of the sick because of the example and command of

Christ. Also, apostolic tradition and church history show the impact that believers have had on the care and healing of the sick. The parable of the Good Samaritan (Luke 10:29-37) and the description of the last judgment (Matt. 25:31-46) both emphasize that to provide for another's needs in the name of Jesus is to minister to the Lord Himself.

With such a biblical basis for visiting the sick it is important that this task and privilege be carried out to the glory of God. The ensuing chapters will seek to inform and instruct the church visitor how to reach that goal.

2

Some Basic Principles

Many church visitors feel uncomfortable in the hospital. This is so partly because many times they assume their duties without a great deal of training and preparation. Most do a very fine job, and through a process of trial and error they eventually work out successful methods of hospital visitation. The basic prerequisite for a successful visit is genuine concern for the patient. If the church visitor is able to communicate this real concern, the visit will be a good experience for all.

Sometimes, even with the best of intentions, the church visitor comes away feeling frustrated and disappointed. It is unlikely that any person, lay or ordained, trained or untrained, will ever feel that his visits are 100-percent effective 100 percent of the time. No course of instruction can guarantee that.

However, there are several basic, fundamental principles that will help the visits to be satisfying to patient and caller alike. These "mechanics" of visitation are suggestive and not exhaustive. Local differences in hospital procedures and protocol will necessitate some adaptation of these basic principles. It may seem that many points are so evident and apparent they do not need inclusion here. But very often disappointments occur when simple factors are ignored.

To the patient the hospital is much like a dormitory bedroom. People come in and out at unpredictable intervals for a variety of reasons. Not only do nurses and physicians come to see the patient, but a host of technicians—not to mention the housekeeper—file in and out of the patient's room. Moreover, very often the room is shared with at least one other patient.

Because of these necessary invasions of the patient's privacy, it is incumbent upon the church visitor to show as much respect for the patient's privacy as possible. Therefore the visit should begin with a light knock on the patient's door. This signals the visitor's presence, but it also gives the patient an opportunity to feel some sense of control. Even if the door is wide open and the patient is able to see who is at the door, it is a distinct courtesy to knock.

The church visitor should be aware that a closed door may indicate several things. It may mean that the patient (or roommate) is resting and does not want to be disturbed. After lightly rapping and getting no response, the church visitor should go on to another room. One should, of course, listen carefully for a bid to enter. The door may be closed only because a humidifier is in use, or because the last person to leave the room inadvertently closed it.

It should also be noted that occasionally the closed door is an indication that the patient is in isolation. When the patient is in isolation a sign to that effect is posted on the door. The visitor should be alert for this and go immediately to the nurses' station for assistance in gowning up and following other precautions. The church visitor should not avoid the patient in isolation simply because of the restrictions, for he may be very receptive to a visit.

Not only should the church visitor be careful to communicate respect for the patient's physical privacy, he should respect privacy of information as well. This means that whatever knowledge one gains about the patient's condition is privileged and sacred. It should stay at the hospital when the visitor leaves. Well-meaning people often ask for information on the patient's condition, but the visitor should not give it out. Discretion at this point is vital. The church visitor could lose all future credibility if confidential material were disclosed.

The church visitor should avoid "pumping" the patient about his condition. Generally the visitor should let the patient take the lead and tell whatever aspects of his illness he wishes to relate. Sometimes the patient finds it helpful to discuss particulars about his physical distress. If so, the visitor should listen actively. But he should beware of communicating an undue interest in this area. Usually it is the patient's feelings about his illness and recovery that are important to explore, not the details of the illness.

As a general rule, the visitor should refrain from relating experiences of others to the patient. For example, if the patient has pneumonia and the visitor himself was recently hospitalized for the same reason, it would be best not to discuss anything about that hospitalization, as it might discourage the patient or give him unrealistic expectations. If the visitor spent only three days in the hospital and the patient has already been in four, it might be demoralizing to the patient, even though he might be progressing quite well.

Further, it is a good rule to say as little about oneself as possible. If the church visitor has any great personal problem, it is a temptation to use the patient as a support. This is grossly unfair to the patient, who is in need of help himself. One should leave personal problems at home when he visits at the hospital. If they are very pressing, then it is well not to come to the hospital at all. One should not use visitation as therapy.

Because the hospitalized patient is generally in a weakened state of health, the church visitor should never come to the hospital if he himself is ill. If he has any cold or flu symptoms and comes to the hospital, it will understandably make the patient uncomfortable. It will come across that the visitor is inconsiderate of the patient's health and well-being.

The church visitor should observe all aspects of good hygiene while in the hospital. This may well involve a good deal of handwashing, but such attention can result only in the good of visitor and patient alike. Infection control is a major concern in all hospitals. The cooperation of the church visitor is mandatory for establishing a good working relationship with the hospital staff.

In this regard it is always appropriate for the church visitor to stop at the nurses' station to identify himself. Often the nurse can give information that will be of help. Of course, unless the church visitor is known by the patient, a personal introduction should be the first order of business. A statement of who the visitor is and why he is there is not only a common courtesy, it also avoids the possible embarrassment of mistaken identity.

Because of the possibility of injury to the patient, the church visitor should not shake the patient's hand. If the patient has had an intravenous or other form of injection in that arm, a handshake could be quite painful. It is best to wait and let the patient extend his hand for greeting first. Even then one should grasp the hand carefully and should not shake it vigorously. Since touch is important in communicating warmth, an alternative to a handshake might be a light touch on the patient's arm or shoulder.

Generally it is a good rule not to sit on the patient's bed, unless the patient requests that the visitor do so. Most hospital rooms have a chair or two that the church visitor can use. Sometimes it is well just to stand in order to maintain eye contact with the patient. The patient should not be made to shift into an uncomfortable position.

The essence of all these small things is that the church visitor "do no harm." Earlier it was pointed out that great potential good can be accomplished by the visitor. The opposite is also true: the church visitor can be of potential harm. If the visit is too long it may tire the patient. The church visitor's interference in any way with the physical care being given can be injurious to the patient.

A hospital call is like a good prayer: it is measured more by depth than by length. One should never overstay, yet it is important not to be brusque. Usually the patient gives the church visitor a cue. Sensitivity to these cues is an important part of the visiting process. If one is to err, it is best to err on the side of brevity. Patients can—and will—ask the visitor to stay a little longer.

Even if the church visitor knows the patient fairly well, he should be careful not to assume the role of nurse or doctor. That is, the visitor must be sure of his role in the hospital and not go beyond it. A drink of water, change of position in bed, candy bar, or cigarette may be contrary to the patient's particular nursing plan. It is always best to check with the nurse before requests for any of these things are met.

For example, if the patient is scheduled for surgery, a drink of water could make him very sick or cause the surgery to be postponed. Changing the patient's position in bed might cause the patient injury—to say nothing of potential injury to the church visitor's back! A candy bar could play havoc with a diabetic's diet, and lighting a cigarette when oxygen is in use might cause an explosion.

To summarize, it has been pointed out that church visitors should not underestimate their impact in the hospital. The potential for both good and harm is great. By observing basic principles of hospital visitation, church visitors can enhance their effectiveness. No amount of training can take the place of a sincere caring for others in time of crisis and tragedy. At the same time, the best of intentions can be misdirected and hampered by a lack of attention to these basic principles.

3

Religion and Health
A Holistic Approach

"Beloved, I pray that all may go well with you and that you may be in health; I know that it is well with your soul" (3 John 2).

The apostle John in these words of greeting reminds us of the interrelationships among mental, physical, and spiritual health. To be completely whole, the mind, body, and spirit must be in tune with each other. At times the desired harmony is disturbed in each of us. Dissonance occurs when illness affects any part of our being. Illness of body will affect the mind and spirit, illness of the mind affects body and spirit, and illness of the spirit affects body and mind. An understanding of this interrelationship is crucial for the church visitor.

Illness (which in this connection is sometimes called unwholeness or fragmentation) begins in body, mind, or spirit, and then spreads to the other two dimensions. This spreading is usually quite rapid. Healing and wholeness occur when all three dimensions are restored to their original functioning. A typical cycle goes something like this: illness or injury afflicts the body; depression follows, affecting the mind; and doubts of God's love then affect the spirit. Or it may occur this way: anger against someone or something upsets the mind, followed by lack of forgiveness, affecting the spirit; this in turn produces physical illness.

In any event the desired equilibrium of spiritual, physical, and mental health is achieved and maintained by continued inter- action of these dimensions. But what is meant or implied when John says, "It is well with your soul"? Spiritual health, like mental and physical health, can be defined in a number of ways. A defini- tion of spiritual wholeness would include at least three compo- nents: acceptance of the love of God, belief in the providence of God, and congruence with the image of God.

Acceptance of the Love of God

God's love is demonstrated in the creation—God so loved He made—and in the incarnation—God so loved He gave. Redeemed humanity, by experiencing God's love, can then reach out and love others. To accept the love of God is to affirm oneself and one's fellow. Man, as an object of God's love, is invested with great dignity and integrity. The church visitor is a representative of the love of God to the hospitalized patient.

The link between God's love and human love is indivisible. One cannot love God and hate his brother (1 John 2:9). In accepting God's love personally, one looks at others in a new perspective. Love binds man not only to God, but to man.

Love seeks the highest good of its object. Love's characteristics are outlined by the apostle Paul (1 Cor. 13); love is the first "fruit of the Spirit" (Gal. 5:22–23). In these contexts love is seen as the core of human relationships.

In order to love others we must accept God's love for us. This involves a conscious choice. We can accept or reject the concept that God is loving. Rejection produces cynicism and existential despair. Life is not good if God is not loving in His relationship to man. In time of pain and suffering the hospitalized patient may tend to lose sight of God's love. The task of the church visitor is to remind the patient of this love.

To see God's love in a world beset by natural disaster and man's inhumanity to man is indeed a "leap of faith," and even more so when personal tragedy and calamity envelop us. If God is love, why does He permit floods, earthquakes, and volcanoes to threaten and destroy human life? If God is loving, why are there not peace on earth and the brotherhood of man? If God is loving, why, a patient might ask, am I hospitalized?

Faith alone can see God's love amid sorrow and suffering. But faith in God's love can be a difficult path to follow in the real world. It is difficult to accept illness when it threatens to separate one from one's family and possessions. The forces of unwholeness and disintegration seem so strong. The ministry of the church visitor is to reinforce the patient's faith.

God's love in the midst of generic and personal tragedy is basically unprovable. And to claim that certain events are the result of His love can be potentially dangerous. To ascribe to God actions which are not His is blasphemous. However, to accept God's love in adversity is therapeutic. Spiritual wholeness in tragedy can be achieved only by accepting God's love.

Loving God does not imply that one insulates himself from natural and human disaster. It does not mean a blind acceptance of one's fate. To accept God's love is to acknowledge that God continually seeks our good in the midst of adversity. A study of the relation between God's love and sovereignty leads into a discussion of trust in God. This is the second ingredient in spiritual wholeness.

Belief in the Providence of God

To be spiritually whole is to have some sense of divine purpose. One's personal view of God's relationship to the universe is crucial. If God is immanent in His creation then the events of one's life are important to God. If God's relationship to the universe terminated with creation, then the events of one's life are of importance only in some existential sense.

The spiritually healthy person must be comfortable with a view of the world that provides a balance between man's will and God's. It seems that extremes should be avoided at this point. An understanding of the will of God that relieves one of any responsibility for his actions is unhealthy. But to assume that only man's own will operates in the universe is to make God irrelevant. Ideally one should accept responsibility for his own actions and deny responsibility for God's.

This is not simple. For example, a man is badly injured in an automobile accident. Is the accident his doing or God's? It could be either, both, or neither. If he is drunk we could say it is the man's fault. If he strikes a tree felled onto the highway by a bolt of lightning, we call that an "act of God." If a drunk driver runs into him, we say neither the injured man nor God is responsible, but the drunk driver.

It is obvious that such attempts to ascribe ultimate responsibility for an accident can be futile at best. Nevertheless, in time of personal tragedy and calamity, the question "Why?" is raised. Somehow it is either comforting or necessary to assign blame or responsibility. The process by which one goes about answering this question indicates the degree of one's spiritual health. Put another way, the question is, "To what extent does God intervene in the course of human history?" The pietist says, "Completely." The humanist says, "Not at all." A healthy balance must be maintained between these extremes. Scripture certainly declares that the hairs of our head are numbered and that God notices the fallen sparrow (Matt. 10:29). Scripture also indicates that some natural events occur in which God apparently does not intervene on a personal basis. Again, trying to ascertain the exact degree of divine intervention can be an exercise in futility.

The spiritually healthy person does not depend upon an exact formulation of God's sovereignty and man's free will. His theology does not aim to put God in a box. He can live with a certain amount of ambiguity. He does not need to know all of the divine mystery. He trusts that each day God will bring him a new awareness and understanding of Himself.

This kind of trust enables one to be open to constant surprise and novelty. It enables one to sustain an awe of God. It frees one from second-guessing God. It is not a brittle faith that cracks when God does something new in one's life. It asks more questions than it can answer. It permeates one's entire life and results in an appreciation of divine purpose in all of life. When one is hospitalized, however, it is obvious his spiritual as well as his physical health is weakened. Then the church visitor will be called upon to facilitate the patient's working through such issues as suffering and sovereignty.

Congruence with the Image of God

A third characteristic of the spiritually healthy person is congruence with the image of God. In creating man in His image and likeness, God confirmed man as the highest order of creation. Man is not like God in physical appearance but in spiritual capacity. To be fully a reflection of God means to be able to respond to

Him. This communication is twofold: to hear God speak and to speak to God.

Prophets and visionaries in all times and places claim to hear God's voice speaking to them. Spiritual wholeness implies a relationship with God so intimate that conversation is natural. Biblical characters such as Abraham and Moses had this kind of contact with God. In New Testament times the risen Lord spoke to men such as Paul and John. In the present time God speaks to those who will listen; He speaks through nature and through written revelation, the Scripture.

The spiritually healthy individual takes pains to stay close to Scripture, for as one moves away from it the voice of God is less clearly discerned. The spiritually healthy individual will not depend upon or expect ecstatic visions and dreams. His relationship to God is so intimate that God gives him a greater understanding of what He has spoken in the Scripture. God gives him spiritual discernment.

In speaking to God the spiritually whole person uses no special vocabulary, no "gimmicks." Prayer becomes a natural outgrowth of a personal relationship. It is an extension of one's self to God. Such praying employs no secret formulas and is characterized by simplicity of thought and word. It is measured more by depth than by length. It asks for nothing but what is consistent with the relationship; it does not demand or cajole.

The effectiveness of such praying is dependent upon the first two dimensions of spiritual health, love and faith. If one accepts the love of God, he can be assured that his prayers will be answered. Faith in God's providential design assures that such answers are in his best interests. Effective prayer results in a spiritual composure that is neither frantic nor demanding.

In such communion with God the sacraments find fulfillment. Service to others is natural and satisfying. A love that gives meaning to both life and death emerges from this kind of relationship to God. Body, mind, and spirit are integrated into one whole person. Health and well-being characterize this kind of unity.

The implications of this chapter for the church visitor are several. First, it is essential that the church visitor have an understanding of the holistic nature of man. Second, the church visitor should have a proper theological perspective in order to examine certain questions with patients. But a word of caution is in order here. Often a patient asks the church visitor, "Why is God permitting my suffering?" At times this question is more an expression of agony than a desire for a theological discourse. Openness and sensitivity on the part of the church visitor will help determine the proper response.

4

Moral Dilemmas in Medicine

Generally speaking, the great advances in medicine that have taken place are related to technology. Medical journals are rife with articles discussing new surgical procedures and equipment. Discussions that deal with moral values are few and infrequent. The physician, as a man of scientific bent and training, sees his role in health as a practitioner. High degrees of technical sophistication have been achieved to the possible neglect of moral issues. This is why the role of the church visitor is so important in the hospital.

To be sure, the church visitor is not an advice giver. However, patients and families may seek to engage the visitor in discussions about decisions they must make. An acquaintance with the issues involved will make the church visitor a more informed listener. He may be able also to help others to a broader understanding of options.

At the heart of moral issues in medicine is the question, If a procedure is medically possible, should it be used? In other words, the application of advanced medical technology is at the core of the problem. Technology is neither good or bad in itself, but its application brings it into the realm and purview of morality.

An example of this might be the use of a respirator. This "breathing machine" performs basic respiration for patients who are not able to breathe for themselves. Its use following heart and lung surgery helps make these procedures possible. Should this

machine, however, be used to perform this vital function indefinitely for a patient who would otherwise be clinically dead? The
use and, to some extent, the length of use of this machine become
moral issues.

This is but one of many moral dilemmas in medicine. This
chapter is not intended to be exhaustive but suggestive of some
principles that may be of use to the church visitor. Discussion,
then, will be limited to two main topics: abortion and prolongation of life. The principles involved in these issues will be sufficient
to illustrate the moral problems which have arisen with the
advent of modern medical technology.

Abortion

Generally an abortion can be performed during the first three
months of pregnancy without medical complications. Using sterile techniques, the procedure offers little or no medical risk. The
fact that an abortion can be done antiseptically, however, has no
bearing on the morality of that act. The rightness or wrongness of
abortion has nothing to do with the state of medical science.

Further, through amniocentesis, congenital birth defects can
be identified in the early weeks of pregnancy. This procedure
involves extracting a small amount of the amniotic fluid which
surrounds the fetus. Analysis of this fluid may indicate abnormal-
ities such as Down's syndrome, or mongolism. Having obtained
this information, the mother may request a therapeutic abortion.

In cases of rape, incest, and threat to the mother's life, the
church's basic opposition to abortion is somewhat relaxed. Each
decision must be reached on an individual basis. The church
visitor must bear in mind that such decisions are personal and
made with information not possessed by him. Therefore an
automatic negative or judgmental attitude is never appropriate.
Even if the church visitor is convinced of the wrongness of the
act, the person visited may not share that conviction.

Whatever the circumstances, an abortion will be likely to produce misgivings and anxieties for the patient and her family. To
be supportive at a time like this is not to condone or approve of
abortion. But it is important to realize that compounding guilt
feelings is not the role of the church visitor at this point.

Many volumes have been written on the ethics of abortion.
Rights of the fetus, rights of the mother, the definition of human

life, legal and biotechnical aspects of abortion—all these issues are involved. Added to these are the social and religious aspects of abortion. Clearly it is a complicated and highly controversial problem. Few people have a sufficient grasp of all the implications to be able to make pronouncements or dictate to others in a particular instance.

What this means is that it is best if the church visitor does not attempt to present his own understanding of what the Scriptures teach about abortion. To be sure, the sacredness of life is a prominent theme in the Bible. But it is possible to retain this conviction and still be uncritical and supportive of others. At the heart of the issue is the meaning of life. Is life itself the only and highest good in all circumstances? Often this is difficult to answer.

Prolongation of Life

At the other extreme of the life cycle is the moral dilemma of the prolongation of life. Again the sacredness and meaning of life are called into question. Here also the church visitor should refrain from giving advice and taking a judgmental stance.

This issue, too, is complicated by the medical technology which can sustain almost any bodily function. Respirators can "breathe" for the patient; dialysis machines can take over kidney functions; and intravenous and nasogastric tubes can supply nourishment to the patient. All these medical wonders are God-given lifesaving devices. The moral problem arises from the length of time these are implemented. In other words, how long should the use of lifesaving equipment be continued?

Let us consider a hypothetical case, the stroke victim. The patient may experience breathing difficulty. Application of the respirator can take over this function until the patient's condition allows him to resume breathing on his own. The problem is one of duration. If the patient is unable to regain his breathing function, should he continue to be hooked up to the respirator? Many issues come into play.

If all other body systems and functions are restored, the continued use of the respirator certainly is appropriate. If, however, the patient is comatose and all other body functions are impaired, use of the respirator becomes a matter of prolonging dying rather than prolonging life. At what precise point should medical efforts be withdrawn, if ever? Scores of papers and books have been written on this issue as well.

The Christian affirmation of life calls for every effort to preserve it as long as some reasonable hope exists for life that is distinctively human. To prolong an existence that could be characterized as vegetative raises serious moral questions. Is it right to sustain a body in this state simply because it is medically and technologically possible to do so?

Few if any persons would desire the sustenance of their physical processes if their spiritual faculties were no longer functioning. That is, most people feel that treating a dead body as if it were a living person is as immoral as treating a living person as though he were already dead. From a Christian perspective the Golden Rule seems a very sensible standard. We should not inflict such an indignity on another that we would not wish for ourselves.

The church visitor again can be very supportive of a family that faces this kind of a moral dilemma. Support in this case means being available and listening carefully to the family. As mentioned above, the family must consider many factors as it faces this difficult decision: the age of the patient, possibility of recovery, extent of damage, expressed wishes of the patient—all these and many more aspects are involved. If the church visitor has some appreciation for the difficulty in making such a decision, he enhances the potential help he can provide.

Very often a subtle trace of guilt surfaces and complicates the situation. Sometimes family members may feel they were not attentive to the patient's needs when he was well. They try to compensate for this by demanding continued heroic medical efforts when such heroics are not warranted. The church visitor should be aware of this possibility when relating to family members. To be a caring presence in such a time of stress is of great help.

Medical advances cover many areas besides those relating to abortion and prolongation of life. Other moral dilemmas that have developed as technology has advanced include such things as organ transplants, genetic engineering, and experimentation on humans. Each of these issues raises ethical questions over which physician, patient, and family ponder and agonize. Many times the persons who must make choices need someone outside the family circle to listen to their deliberations. By listening intelligently and sympathetically, the church visitor may be able to facilitate the sometimes agonizing process.

5

The Hospital Environment

An appreciation of the unique character of the hospital environment is helpful, if not indispensable, for the church visitor. In order to empathize with the patient, an understanding of what being in the hospital means is necessary. Patients can quickly discern whether the church visitor really knows what it is like to be hospitalized. An important part of establishing rapport lies in letting the patient know that his perception of hospitalization is shared by most other patients.

To be sure, there is nothing like a hospital. Comparisons have been made to a small town, an aircraft carrier, and a university. Probably each of these similes has an element of truth. On any given day a hospital may have as many patients and staff as a community. The organization, chain of command, and self-containment resemble that of a large ship. Further, the bureaucracy, departmental infighting, and learning that occur in universities also take place in the hospital.

Like other social institutions, the hospital is more than the sum of its parts. In the hospital, life begins and ends, people are healed because of or in spite of medical intervention, hopes are affirmed and denied, knowledge is disseminated, and important moral and ethical decisions are made. Patients are the focus of all this activity.

Generally patients are reluctant to enter the hospital and eager to leave. A hospital chaplain was heard to say, "I sometimes feel like a prison chaplain: nobody wants to come in, and everybody wants to get out!" The church visitor will appreciate the predominance of negative feelings expressed by patients.

Basically, then, the distinctive feeling produced by the hospital environment is a sense of loss, a feeling of depersonalization and disorientation. Granted, a new mother may feel that her stay in the hospital was productive, but most hospital experiences are not that positive. Most patients may feel that health is gained; however, in achieving this goal one experiences this sense of loss. A number of reasons for this feeling will be noted here.

Admission

Usually admission to the hospital is in itself an acknowledgment that good health and wholeness have been lost or threatened. Whether the medical condition is temporary or chronic, the experience of being admitted to the hospital is one of loss. This trauma is heightened by the very language used in the routine admission procedure, as well as by some of the procedures themselves. Personal information such as one's marital status and age is "taken." X rays are "taken." Blood is "drawn"; urine is "collected"; personal effects and clothing are replaced by hospital stock.

Unintentionally these things all contribute to a patient's feeling of depersonalization. Name bands and admission numbers heighten this feeling. Personal identity and integrity seem to be under attack. Thus the church visitor can be very helpful simply by affirming the personhood of the patient and by being a friend. At a time when the patient feels more like a number than an individual person, it is important for the church visitor to be there.

Loss of Responsibility

Admission to the hospital signals to both family and community that the patient is automatically released from the usual responsibilities of home and work. This may be a mixed blessing. On the one hand it is a relief to the patient to be free from the ordinary demands of family relationships. However, if the patient's home relationships are already strained, the stress of hospitalization may well intensify them. This is why the church visitor may need to minister to the family as well as to the patient.

The same is true of job-related responsibility. If the illness is a result of the patient's employment, simply to be away from work may be therapeutic. On the other hand, being away from the job may cause anxiety and stress. The church visitor may wish to explore the possibility of job problems with the patient and let the patient talk about work and ventilate any negative feelings about it.

The issue in each case is the amount of control the patient feels is lost due to hospitalization. A dependent person may well welcome the fact that his condition hinders or prevents a take-charge posture. For the independent person such limitations are in themselves stress-producing and may complicate the healing process. Ideally the patient should take an active role with the physician in treatment of and recovery from illness, but he should still be cooperative and compliant with the physician's recommendations for their mutually acceptable therapy plan.

Too often the patient feels overwhelmed by hospitalization and perceives everything negatively. The church visitor should be aware of this and help the patient express these feelings. So much of what the patient experiences is beyond his control. Meal times and menu selection are often dictated by test schedules and dietetic regimen rather than patient choice. Perhaps the reason that many patients do not eat properly is that not eating is a form of control on their part. Stubborn and uncooperative behavior may also be interpreted in this light. Patients themselves may be unaware of these dynamics, but the church visitor should consider this possibility.

Loss of Privacy

Hospitalization is like opening the doors of one's bedroom to the public. Not only physicians and nurses walk in and out of the patient's room, but a host of technicians as well. It is little wonder that the patient feels somewhat awkward and uncomfortable in the hospital setting. Clad in nightclothes, the patient's body is often somewhat exposed; its functions are watched closely and charted. Urinals and bedpans are always present. This lack of privacy often contributes to the stress of hospitalization. The church visitor should be cognizant of these feelings and accord the patient as much privacy as possible. To this end, more listening than questioning would be in order.

Lack of Information

Not only does the hospitalized patient feel that his privacy is exploited, he also feels that much information and knowledge is kept from him. What seems like a conspiracy among hospital staff makes the patient tense and nervous. He often feels he is the last to know about his condition. However, usually patients want information about themselves that is not available; that is, the physician may still be in the process of assembling data and test results. Patients assume that the x-ray technician or escort knows the results of the x ray immediately or that the lab technician can immediately interpret their blood test.

To feel that one is uninformed may produce a degree of anger and hostility. The church visitor can help by supplying some information to the patient. This does not mean information about the patient's condition, but about general medical procedure. The church visitor may enhance his effectiveness by sharing his knowledge of medical and hospital routine, which may not be obvious to the patient. For example, to explain to a patient why he should not drink water immediately before surgery may indeed help the patient accept such an order more easily. In fact, often procedures are explained to patients by a staff member, but in their anxiety such information may be forgotten or confused.

Certainly the church visitor is not a physician, nurse, or patient educator, but whatever accurate information can be given is helpful. The danger, of course, is that the church visitor may forget his role and assume a different one. The church visitor is not primarily an educator or advocate, but a friend and support. If the patient needs more than that the church visitor should be aware of available referral services.

Probably the greatest anxiety for the hospital patient is fear of the unknown. Whatever the patient's condition is upon admission, it is hoped that that condition will be improved by being in the hospital. Even as people are hesitant to go to the dentist until a toothache is almost unbearable, so they often postpone going to the doctor and the hospital as well. This often complicates conditions that are best treated as soon as possible. For this reason the church visitor may generally expect patients to feel a certain amount of guilt and self-blame.

To many people, admission to the hospital is a personal defeat. They identify the hospital more in terms of failure to avoid sickness than in terms of attempting to stay well. Older persons often see the hospital as a place to die rather than to get well. Such negative feelings do not evaporate upon admission but rather increase. Helping patients identify some of the reasons for their anxiety about being in the hospital can be extremely valuable. The church visitor can assist in this process as the patient's listening friend.

In summary, it has been noted that people feel they lose their personal identity when they become hospital patients. This loss of individuality is usually accompanied by a loss of control and independence, and is exacerbated by a loss of privacy and sense of dignity. The church visitor can be of great assistance in alleviating the effects of this subtractive process. According the patient full personhood, affirming his worth as a child of an unchanging God, and showing respect for his wishes and personal needs can help reverse these feelings of loss. The hospital is indeed a unique environment; the church visitor can supply a unique service.

6

Relationships
with the Hospital Staff

Without question the contemporary hospital is the province or "turf" of the medical arts. Physician, nurse, and technologist all have a medical orientation. The church visitor must appreciate this reality, but should not be intimidated by it. The church visitor's ministry to hospital patients should never be underestimated or discounted. Recognition of the roles of and relationships among the hospital staff can enhance this ministry.

Several groups of hospital staff will be dealt with in this chapter: physicians, nurses, technicians, and other personnel. Hospital personnel should always be accorded courtesy and respect if the church visitor is to expect the same from them. Each group has a job to do in the hospital that will directly or indirectly affect the patient. Other hospital employees such as housekeepers may affect the patient as well. However, the doctors, nurses, and technicians will be the dominant people during the patient's stay.

Physicians

In a real sense the physician is at the head of the hospital team. He gives orders for patient care to the nurse and orders and interprets the tests the technician conducts. To the patient the physician is the most important individual in the hospital. The physician admits and discharges; he is ultimately responsible for the patient's progress. Usually the physician makes daily rounds and assesses the patient's needs.

Patients relate to their physician (or their primary one, if there are several) in a variety of ways. Some adopt a very docile, dependent role; others may be critical and demanding. The church visitor can discern patients' attitudes fairly easily.

The church visitor should not pass judgment on the medical care the patient is receiving. That is, he should not cause the patient to lose confidence in or question the physician's expertise. At the same time, if the church visitor has serious questions about a patient's medical care, he may want to contact the pastor or family, but he should not bring up the matter to the patient.

Ideally the church visitor will work with the physician in supporting the patient. If the patient has no close family the church visitor may function as a liaison between the patient and physician. Most physicians will appreciate the role and contribution of the church visitor at this point. Information that the visitor can give about the patient and the patient's family situation may be helpful to the physician in the devising of plans for treatment and discharge.

Nurses

In most cases the patient has more contact with the nurses than with his physician. Doctors are perceived as being busy; thus the patient often feels more comfortable talking to his nurse. In many larger hospitals nurses are so specialized that the patient sees several nurses, some of them for only a short period of time. For instance, a nurse may come in only to start an intravenous injection. Even then, however, nurses seem more approachable than physicians.

Nurses often feel squeezed between the doctor and the patient. Physicians dictate a treatment plan and the nurse is obligated to see that it is carried out. The patient sometimes does not cooperate with the treatment plan and resists the nurse's efforts to implement it. The nurse is in the middle and may have to placate both. Church visitors should be aware of this and help patients understand the nurses' position a little better.

Because the nurse is entrusted with the day-by-day care of the patient, she is concerned with all aspects of the patient's progress.

Most nurses see the church visitor as an important aid to the patient's recovery. It is helpful to the nurse if the church visitor respects her responsibility and checks with her about the patient's condition. A brief stop at the nurses' station or a few words with the nurse in the hall is extremely important. She can indicate any aspect of the patient's situation that might affect the visit.

For example, if the patient has just received an injection to relieve pain, he may not be as alert and responsive as he usually is. The church visitor should be sensitive to the patient's needs and assure the nurse that the anticipated visit will be brief and not exhausting to the patient. Occasionally nurses will advise against a visit at a particular time. The church visitor will want to abide by this judgment as being in the best interest of the patient.

The nurse will be a great ally of the church visitor when assured that the patient's interest is foremost. One of the values of making regular visits to the hospital is that nurses and other hospital personnel will recognize the church visitor as one who can be trusted to pursue the patient's good. Such trust is not automatically conferred, but must be earned.

Technicians

Another group of hospital personnel that the church visitor should be aware of is the technicians. These include physical and respiratory therapists as well as x-ray and laboratory technicians. Each of the departments these people represent receives orders from the physician to assist in the diagnostic and therapeutic aspects of patient care. In some cases these people will play an important and significant part in the patient's recovery. They may actually be perceived to be as beneficial to the patient's progress as is the physician himself. An example of this might be the physical therapist who teaches an accident victim to regain the use of a limb.

These technicians are often seen as more approachable than either physician or nurse, and a strong relationship may develop with the patient. Their encouragement and help may favorably affect the patient's morale and attitude. For the church visitor this means that the patient's schedule may include sessions with these technicians that are very meaningful to the patient. Their time, like that of the physician and nurse, is frequently tightly scheduled and should be respected by the church visitor. In other words, the church visitor should be prepared to defer his visits or abbreviate them for the good of the patient.

Others

The typical hospital staff includes a host of other personnel. Each of these has a special function to perform. Sometimes these duties bring them into patient contact. For example, a house-keeper may develop rapport with a long-term patient that could be quite helpful and therapeutic. Whatever the nature of the contact, the patient may be significantly affected.

The church visitor will do well to be sensitive to all hospital staff and to appreciate each one's unique contribution to patient care. Usually it is courteous, if not mandatory, for the church visitor to ask if he should excuse himself when any hospital personnel enter the room in which he is visiting. This prevents any embarrassment on anyone's part, and the church visitor thus avoids being asked to leave the patient's room. Generally hospital personnel will make every effort not to interrupt the patient and any visitor. Sometimes, however, it is necessary, even during stated visiting hours.

It will always be advantageous for the church visitor to co-operate with the entire hospital staff as much as possible. Every hospital probably has a different departmental organization, but physicians, nurses, and technicians are always in plain view. The church visitor can enhance the effectiveness of his ministry by becoming familiar with the structure and working with it.

If, for instance, the patient has some anxiety about his financial needs, it is extremely helpful to know where to refer for help. Financial counselors, social-service workers, and business-office personnel may be able to give assistance if alerted to the need. The church visitor may wish to contact the dietitian about the patient's menu if the patient comments on it. In short, the hospital probably has the personnel to address any of the patient's needs. The church visitor can render valuable service to all concerned by being familiar with the entire hospital staff. Being an effective liaison between the patient and hospital personnel is a decided plus for the dedicated church visitor.

PART TWO

General Patient Visitation

7

Meeting the Unexpected

To serve as a church visitor is one of the most gratifying experiences a person can have. However, as this commitment requires direct patient contact, a certain risk is involved. The risk comes when the church visitor encounters patients' unexpected and sometimes unpleasant reactions. The purpose of this chapter is to discuss some of the situations which might produce discomfort for the church visitor. Four types of patients will be considered: the angry patient, the unresponsive patient, the dying patient, and the immodest patient.

The Angry Patient

When a patient is admitted to the hospital, he brings his entire person, not just a sick body. The wide variety of human nature dictates that some persons' emotional release will take the form of anger. Hospitalization implies loss: loss of health, of body function and control, of self-image, of usual relationships. All of these losses combine to threaten the patient's ego. Some patients respond to the stress of hospitalization with hostility. This means that when a church visitor comes into direct contact with patients, he may meet one who will respond angrily.

One of the first things we all do when we encounter anger is to react defensively. When meeting a hostile patient, we may react by reexplaining our position or our role, by getting angry at the patient, or by withdrawing from him. It is not pleasant to react

45

this way. Compounding the difficulty is the high motivation of most church visitors to help others. The angry patient says that he does not appreciate that help.

The danger is that the church visitor may internalize the anger expressed—that is, become angry himself—or take it personally. Ideally, instead of reacting defensively the church visitor should understand the source of the patient's anger. To realize that the hostility is the patient's reaction to his circumstances and not a personal affront to the church visitor is the first step in dealing with negative feelings. As mentioned above, the patient's anger at needing to be in the hospital may be displaced and directed toward the church visitor.

There are other possible sources of a patient's hostile reaction. The patient may have entered the hospital with mild or moderate apprehension. Then if bad news comes unexpectedly, rage may well be exhibited. The patient who expects a diagnosis of stomach flu and finds out instead that he has a malignant tumor will be enraged. Such a patient may be angry at the church visitor, who seems healthy and happy while the patient is feeling sick and depressed.

Again it must be stressed that it is nothing the church visitor has said or done that touches off such an explosion of anger. It is not as if the church visitor could have said or done something else. Happily this kind of patient reaction is not frequent. But it does happen. It is important that the church visitor have some insight into the causes of the patient's anger.

Another source of patient anger is pain. Most people are grouchy when they are not feeling well. Anyone can be short of temper when he has a splitting headache. This is often the case in the hospital when a postsurgical patient is between shots to relieve pain. Many procedures done in the hospital cause some degree of pain and discomfort. Furthermore, some tests and most surgeries are performed after a patient has fasted for a number of hours. Being hungry and thirsty makes the patient irritable at best and angry at worst.

Whatever the source—and church visitors may never know—angry expressions may be directed at them. Rather than become defensive or discouraged, however, one must try to gain some appreciation of the feelings of the angry patient. This is the beginning of empathy. Church visitors who cannot develop empathy for patients should not be working in a position requiring patient contact.

The Unresponsive Patient

Another type of patient encountered by the church visitor is the unresponsive patient, who cannot communicate or respond appropriately. Some patients, it is evident, would like to communicate but cannot, whereas others seem to look at the visitor without indicating they are aware of his presence. The church visitor will discover this problem when he asks a question or makes a comment, and receives no indication that the patient has heard or understood. We live in a verbal society and expect the hospital will prove no exception. It is easy to become frustrated when a patient with whom one is seeking to communicate does not respond appropriately or at all. As with the angry patient, it will be helpful to examine some possible reasons that the unresponsive patient is unable to communicate.

Basically most patients who do not communicate with the church visitor are unable to do so. They probably are not able to communicate with the hospital personnel either. Church visitors should not automatically assume that they have made an error in attempting to visit with this type of patient, even though communication seems impossible. It is difficult not to assume so because we rely heavily upon verbal feedback for affirmation of ourselves. Two-way communication is a validation of our ministry.

This inability to communicate may be due to several causes. Some of these are obvious. For example, the patient who usually wears a hearing aid may not be able to have it in place because of a medical procedure (such as preoperative preparation). Unless the patient is facile in lip reading, the church visitor may get an inappropriate response or none at all. Should such a patient be encountered, the church visitor may wish to give the patient an opportunity to communicate by written word.

In some locales language differences may be a factor. In the southwestern United States Indian and Spanish patients are common. Patients from other countries may have difficulty with verbal communication because of a language barrier. However, this may not be obvious to the church visitor on an initial contact.

Medical conditions may also make communication difficult. A classic instance is the patient who has had a stroke that results in temporary aphasia. This inability to speak is as frustrating to the patient as to the church visitor and may be accompanied by the patient's spontaneous sobbing. (Fuller discussion of the stroke patient will follow in chapter 16.)

Patients who have been sedated may be very slow to respond. The church visitor will need to be very understanding of this condition and be willing to spend additional time, if necessary, with the patient. Some medical procedures, such as a bronchoscopy, may result in a patient's temporary inability to talk because of swollen throat tissue. As mentioned above, written communication is a viable alternative.

On rare occasions a psychiatric patient who has an acute medical problem will be placed in one of the general areas of the hospital. A patient with a mental condition such as autism or catatonia will be unable to communicate. Generally any effort to relate to such a patient will be ineffective.

The church visitor will need to bear in mind that in the hospital he will come across the patient who cannot communicate. Knowing this the church visitor will be protected from unwarranted negative feelings when such a patient is encountered.

The Terminal Patient

Although medical personnel are dedicated to the art and science of healing, their best efforts cannot stave off the inevitability of death. Although terminal patients are sent home whenever possible, the church may have occasion to visit them in the hospital. This can cause the church visitor extreme anxiety for several reasons.

One cause of anxiety is identification with the patient. That is, the dying patient may be the same age and sex as the church visitor. This produces the reaction, "This could be me!" It is always threatening to be reminded of our own mortality. Since it is difficult to separate feelings of empathy and identification, some church visitors may find it impossible to deal meaningfully with such patients.

The same feeling may occur when the terminal patient is the same age and sex as a member of the church visitor's immediate family. Anxiety attends the forceful realization, "This could be my spouse (or child)!" It is important to realize, however, that identification is a completely normal reaction.

Another source of anxiety for the visitor in relating to the terminal patient is those occasions when the patient wishes to discuss his death and its meaning. The church visitor may feel very uncomfortable when a patient says, "I've got terminal cancer," or "I am not going to get well." The usual response is to say, "You might be one of the lucky ones," or "Sure, you're going to get well." There is a natural tendency to cut off a discussion we feel is threatening to us. To talk about death is to discuss the ultimate threat.

On the other hand, talk about death may cause the patient anxiety. That is, the church visitor may feel comfortable discussing mortality with the dying patient, but the patient may not want to talk about it. The church visitor may feel that the patient is denying the facts and being harmfully unrealistic. In such cases the patient's feelings have to be considered, and it is generally best not to pursue such a discussion further.

In relating to the terminal patient the church visitor should have a strong awareness of his own feelings. Unless this is the case, a helpful exchange of ideas is not possible. Accompanying this self-awareness should be the ability to accept the ideas and concepts of the patient even if they seem inappropriate to the visitor. To know our own feelings and to be able to accept the feelings of others is a good combination to bring to any human encounter.

The Immodest Patient

Hospital personnel make every effort to protect the privacy and integrity of each patient. This extends to preventing physical exposure as well. However, there may be isolated and infrequent occasions when the church visitor comes upon a patient who is inadequately covered.

Usually a patient who is inadequately covered is under sedation. A patient immediately before or after surgery, for example, may kick off his bed covers—and hospital gowns are not designed with patient modesty in mind! It is likely the church visitor will feel anxious and uncomfortable, particularly if the patient is of the opposite sex. Probably the best response is to leave the patient's room and inform the floor nurse assigned to that patient.

Such occurrences are quite rare, but they do happen. The other type of immodesty encountered is, fortunately, even rarer. This is when the patient is deliberate in his lack of modesty. Unfortunately some patients' anxiety about their masculinity or femininity may be expressed in this way. The church visitor will feel uncomfortable and abused in these instances, but such patients are not likely to attempt any overt action. The response should be the same: inform the patient's nurse. Indifference is a better response to such patients than are expressions of disgust. The church visitor should realize, even though it is difficult, that such a patient needs counseling or some form of psychotherapy, not condemnation.

These, then, are four categories of patients to whom the church visitor may occasionally relate. Most experiences of visiting in the hospital are very positive and satisfying. The encounters described in this chapter happen infrequently. Nonetheless, to be aware that such occurrences may take place will be an asset for the church visitor.

8

The Terminal Patient

Although dealt with briefly in the previous chapter, the terminal patient merits a fuller discussion. This type of patient will be encountered with greater regularity than hostile, unresponsive, or immodest patients. The church visitor can be of great support to the terminally ill patient and family members.

Research on terminally ill patients has been relatively recent. Although others have contributed to this field, much of the data has been collected by Elisabeth Kübler-Ross, a Swiss psychiatrist. Her book, *On Death and Dying* (Macmillan, 1969), has become very popular in the helping professions. The five stages of grief described here are based on her work.

Often there is a reluctance to visit the terminal patient. The church visitor may feel some sense of awkwardness; "I don't know what to say" is a common remark. It should be noted that part of the awkwardness felt in relating to terminal patients comes from the inability to accept one's own mortality. In a very real sense, every patient is terminally ill and every human being is mortal. Truly, "it is appointed for men to die once" (Heb. 9:27).

What this means is that the church visitor should not pity the terminal patient, for the visitor will certainly encounter the same destiny. Furthermore, for the same reason the church visitor should not feel smug or superior to the terminal patient. We share a common humanity with the terminal patient. Often our feelings of awkwardness stem from a process of identification. That is, the dying patient may be the same age as we ourselves or

51

as one of our family members. To realize that "that could be me" is a sobering thought indeed. Only if the church visitor is confident in his own relationship to God can he be of help to the dying patient.

This chapter will consist of a discussion of the five stages of grief and ways in which the church visitor can best deal with them. This will be followed by a discussion of eight key concepts that may be of help when dealing with terminal patients and their families.

Stages of Grief

It should be pointed out that this formulation of the grieving process is not definitive. It may be helpful in relating to the dying patient, but it should not be superimposed on every patient or seen as an inevitable model. Not all patients will experience or express their feelings in this way or order. Therefore this discussion should be viewed as a possible guide but not as an inflexible progression.

Denial

Denial is generally observed during the early or diagnostic stage of illness. Typically a patient who receives an unfavorable diagnosis will feel that some mistake has been made in the test results, that perhaps he has gotten the test results of some other patient. The reality of a serious illness is denied. This denial may be reflected in a very casual attitude or possibly in excessive humor.

As a defense mechanism, denial gives the patient time to adjust to the unthinkable—that one is mortal after all. The exact impact of this realization is affected by the age of the patient. It is possible that a younger patient may need to use denial more extensively than an aged patient. Most patients after an initial period of denial shift into another stage in the grieving process. A few, it seems, indulge in denial to the extent of delusion.

The church visitor needs to be aware of how to handle this stage of the process. While it might seem desirable to help a patient accept a painful reality, a confrontational stance is not advised. It may be that a better approach would be to share the shock with the patient, at least initially. One approach to the patient might be, "It doesn't seem real. . . ." Often this is a very honest way to begin, since the patient may seem to be in good health. It signals to the patient that the church visitor is likewise shattered at the bad news the patient has received. It is important to the patient to feel that others perceive an abhorrent situation in the same light.

In other words, the church visitor should not try to talk the patient out of his denial at this time. That may only serve to distance the church visitor from the patient. Usually the patient comes to deal with the unpleasant reality in his own time.

The church visitor may encounter a denial reaction from the patient's family as well. As in a time of sudden, unexpected death or other shock, this reaction is almost always present. At times the patient's family needs ministry as much or more than the patient. The church visitor's support of the family is often another way of ministering to the patient.

Anger

Following denial, the patient will often enter a hostile period. For the church visitor this means that the patient may express anger at him, the church, and God. It is not hard to understand the terminal patient's frustration and feeling of futility. Again this will usually be more observable in a younger person. For the elderly, death often comes as a friend rather than foe. The younger person's love and zest for life are expressed in anger.

Understanding this, the church visitor must not take the patient's angry acts or words in a personal, defensive way. Care must be taken at this point not to alienate the terminal patient by reacting to him in anger. Ministry, to be effective, must be accepting of the terminal patient's emotional outbursts as a natural reaction to an ultimately disastrous circumstance. The church visitor should guard against a self-righteousness that imputes guilt to the patient. Forgiveness should be at the forefront of the relationship.

Anger expressed at the church and God should be seen in the same light. The church visitor need not assume a defensive stance regarding the church. Although the patient's anger at the church may be misdirected and excessive, it is usually better for the church visitor to be accepting.

Anger against God somehow seems blasphemous, and the church visitor may be prone to try to prevent or restrict the patient's anger in this direction. But reading the lament of Job illustrates that God is well able to vindicate Himself; the church visitor need not assume God's role. A possible response to the terminal patient at this stage might be, "It doesn't seem fair. . . ."

As with denial, this emotional phase may be experienced by the family also. The church visitor should be aware of the opportunity to minister to the family at this time. Grief is such a powerful emotion that family members may say things they will regret later. If the church visitor reacts defensively, he might possibly alienate the family from the church and God. By being accepting and enabling the family to understand this stage of the grieving process, the church visitor will help them adjust to the loss they experience.

Bargaining

This third stage is apparent when the patient accepts the reality of his situation and is no longer angry, but expresses a desire to negotiate. Usually it is a case of wanting to do or see something that is of great importance to the patient. For example, the patient may accept the inevitability of his death, but hope that a birthday, anniversary, graduation, or wedding of some family member may be experienced first. Often there is an unspoken contract with God.

The church visitor should be aware of what is happening here. Patients may wish to involve the church visitor in these special events. A response the visitor could make might be, "I hope you can. . . ." The danger of bargaining is seen in the so-called foxhole conversion, in which an individual promises to do the will of God if God will spare his life. The patient may genuinely intend to do something God wants if he realizes his wish. Job, for example, wanted to "reason" with God.

It may be necessary for the church visitor to minister to the patient's disappointment if such "bargains" aren't consummated. To identify God's love correctly in a time of apparent loss is difficult indeed. It is important to support the patient in his desires, yet help him accept the limitation imposed by his illness. Again the church visitor should be attentive to the patient's family, who may engage in bargaining activities of their own.

Depression

It is hard to imagine grieving without depression. This is the most universal and pervasive element in the grief process. Usually the depression centers on some element of loss such as loss of a relationship or loss of the familiar. Such depression is not abnormal or un-Christian, unless indulged in for an excessive period of time. The church visitor may find depression difficult to relate to. Reacting to depression by attempting to "cheer the patient up" is more well intentioned than effective. Usually such attempts depress the patient further.

To be most helpful to the depressed patient, the church visitor should allow the patient to own these deep feelings of loss as being legitimate and real. Rather than trying to talk the patient out of his depression, it is best for the visitor to let the patient know that he shares a portion of the loss. The church visitor's response may need be only a simple "I'm sorry."

Ministry to the family in a time of loss involves helping them cope with depression. Again an assurance that to feel "down" is very appropriate and not un-Christian is in order. However, in a time of bereavement many well-intentioned people may say to a family member, "I know how you feel." Such a statement presumes that a similar loss was experienced. It is generally poor judgment to make such a statement, since every relationship is special and unique. Saying this to one who is grieving over a significant loss may seem to be insensitive and insincere. We really do not know how another feels about his loss. It is better for the church visitor to say nothing than to come across as either unknowing or uncaring.

Acceptance

It is doubtful whether anyone really accepts the reality of his own death. It might be more accurately described as resignation. Even genuinely victorious Christians who face death with great faith usually come to this point with some lingering regrets. Because we are not perfect in our living it is not likely that we will be perfect in our dying.

The church visitor should appreciate this and not attempt to force the terminal patient toward an unrealistic emotion or attitude. Even the apostle Paul, who firmly believed that "to live is Christ, and to die is gain," had strong feelings about remaining in the flesh on account of the Philippian church (Phil. 1:21, 24). Later on, as his life drew to a close, Paul seemed much less ambivalent, more reconciled to dying, as when he wrote, "I have fought

the good fight, I have finished the race, I have kept the faith"
(2 Tim. 4:7).

Most persons have some sense of "unfinished business" when
faced with a terminal illness. The church visitor can be of help if
he understands this and does not censure the patient whose
acceptance of death comes slowly if at all.

Key Concepts

The following eight concepts are offered as help to the church
visitor relating to the terminal patient and his family. Each of
these thoughts must be conveyed in the church visitor's own
language and adapted to any specific patient or situation (in
some cases these are intended to help the family after the patient
has died). Not all will seem appropriate to use for all patients or
family members. For the most part they will be useful for the
Christian patient and family.

1. Love is eternal and stronger than death (Jer. 31:3; Song of
Sol. 8:6). Death does not end the love we have for our family. Love
abides (1 Cor. 13:13). The unending character of love can be of
great comfort in time of terminal illness and death.

2. A corollary of this is that the separation caused by death will
be temporary. God promises reunion and resurrection. Death is
the vehicle by which the believer is ushered into eternity. The
result of sin, death is a natural event that comes to all. The pain
of separation is real, however, even though people will be re-
united. Often the church visitor will hear a surviving spouse say
something like, "I wish God would take me, too." Usually this is
more an expression of sorrow than a suicidal gesture. Rather
than responding to the statement directly, a response to the feeling of sadness which prompted it would be more appropriate.
Perhaps it would be helpful to say, "You were very close and I'm
sorry you'll miss him so much."

The assurance of resurrection is one of the most helpful
themes in assisting a person through the grieving process. To
know that life does not end with physical death is to have a hope
that sustains and comforts.

3. The loss will be very painful for the survivors. In one sense
human life is a series of losses up to and including death, the
ultimate loss. Many losses in the course of human life are tem-
pered by gains or substitutions for our losses. However, in death

there is no offsetting gain. The church visitor, then, should never tell parents of a deceased child that having another child will take the place of the one they lost. Children are never replaceable.

This is not to say that death is the worst thing that can happen. Nonetheless, the church visitor needs to be aware that remarks like "He is better off now" or "It is a blessing that she is finally at peace" are best made by the immediate family only. That is, although a person may find comfort in the realization that a loved one is no longer in pain, for the church visitor to verbalize this may come across as being insensitive and impersonal.

4. Loneliness produces depression and withdrawal. As mentioned above, survivors as well as the terminal patient are prone to depression. At the death of a spouse the survivor may suddenly feel like half a person, since Scripture says that in the marriage union two become one. In the void and vacuum created by the death of a loved one the church visitor can be of immeasurable help. To ease the adjustment to widowhood (or widowerhood), the church visitor may need to insist at some point that the surviving spouse attend a church social function with him.

Loneliness and self-pity easily develop in the grieving process. Drawing out the grieving into the world of the living may be traumatic for all concerned, but is necessary. The church visitor should not feel that the survivor is doing well simply because he handled the funeral experience in apparently good grace. Just as one of the great fears of the terminal patient is abandonment, so the survivors fear being forsaken and uncared for.

5. It is almost inevitable that family members will develop some feelings of guilt, since we are not perfect in any human relationship. Whether the terminal patient is a child or adult, family members share a sense of guilt. Too often the patient dies before everything that the family wished to say or do is properly taken care of. Real or exaggerated guilt may prolong and complicate the grieving process. The church visitor will hear feelings of guilt expressed in such ways as "If only I would have . . ." or "I knew I shouldn't have. . . ."

To help both the terminally ill patient and the family make adjustments, the church visitor may suggest that part of the reason we do what we should not and fail to do what we should is our humanity and finitude. Only Christ Himself was blameless in all relationships. To presume that we should be as perfect as He is theologically dangerous.

6. It is acceptable to doubt, question, and be angry at God. As we indicated above, in the stress of terminal illness the patient and family may experience anger. The church visitor will pick up on this feeling in the question, "What did I do that God is punishing me like this?" or the statement, "I prayed so hard that I would be healed, but now the doctor gives no hope at all." Sometimes when such language is used, the church visitor will need to determine if the patient and family really want to talk about the ways of God in time of illness or whether they are pleading for empathy and understanding. Again the church visitor should be aware of the emotion behind the question as well as the content of the question or statement itself. Persons should not be made to feel that it is wrong to think in these terms. The Book of Job indicates that Job in his uprightness asked these same kinds of questions. Christ in His agony asks, "My God, My God, why hast thou forsaken me?" (Matt. 27:46). God understands these outcries of grief and pain.

7. We do not fully understand God's ways and the suffering that is unique to the individual. To admit that we are limited in our knowledge of God is strength. Giving glib or simplistic answers to the deepest questions of human existence is of no benefit to anyone. The church visitor should not feel that complete answers are necessary (or possible) when dealing with human tragedy. The fact is that the righteous suffer and the wicked prosper at times for reasons we do not fully comprehend. To share our awe of the wisdom and power of God with the patient and family can be of help.

8. God shares our grief; He enters into our world of suffering. Christ endured suffering so that as a great high priest He could minister effectively to those who suffer. The church visitor should communicate to the patient and family an assurance of God's abiding presence in time of need. This is accomplished not only by words but also by deeds. As an ambassador of Christ the church visitor attests to God's care and presence by being there and showing concern. Because of the visitor's awkwardness in seeing the terminal patient, too often the patient receives less attention than improving patients. The church visitor will soon realize that a caring presence is far more helpful than pious phrases.

Dealing with the terminally ill patient and his family offers a unique opportunity to the church visitor. Familiarity with the usual phases in the grief process will be invaluable in under-standing and responding to the needs and reactions of the patient and family. The eight concepts suggested here may also be helpful to the church visitor. Perhaps at no other time should the care and concern of other Christians be more evident than in visiting the terminal patient and his family.

9

The Surgical Patient

As in other areas of medical advance, surgical procedures have been greatly improved. This is reflected in shorter hospital stays as well as less time spent in surgery. Improvement is seen also in anesthesia, which is more efficient and has fewer side effects than previously. The church visitor can legitimately assure a patient who has never had surgery (or who has not had surgery within the past twenty years) that things will probably go better than the patient anticipates. Surgical patients are usually sitting on the side of the bed or up walking the day following the procedure.

A current trend is the establishment of day surgery units within the hospital or free-standing facilities where many less complicated procedures are done. This is a great saving to the patient in both time and money. Another trend is the development of new surgical procedures. Coronary bypass surgery is hardly twenty years old. Heart transplants are being attempted with more frequency and greater success. Laser beams in surgery (as in retinal detachment repair) are being used. Body scanners can pinpoint areas of the proposed surgery and indicate potential problems.

With all these advances and improvements the church visitor may think that surgical patients have no spiritual needs at all. Obviously this is not true. Actually surgical patients may well have more anxiety than others. The amount of fear and uncertainty varies according to the type of surgery and how this surgery is perceived by the patient. This chapter will examine five categories of surgical procedures, subtractive, corrective, cosmetic, exploratory, and emergency, and will indicate the role of the church visitor for each type of surgery. These divisions are somewhat arbitrary; that is, there may be some overlap of categories.

Subtractive Surgery

Subtractive surgery involves the loss of some body part or function. Such loss is usually perceived as negative by the surgical patient. An example of such surgery is the amputation of any extremity. Since society places such emphasis on physical perfection, there is usually some type of depressive reaction. Even if the affected limb is gangrenous and painful, its amputation is traumatic. One's self-image is profoundly affected by such surgery. This is not to say that the patient does not intellectually acknowledge the benefits of the operation. Still, he feels sadness that a part of his person is somehow permanently lost.

The church visitor should emphasize that our wholeness before God is not contingent upon our being physically "complete." Being a real person is a function of the spirit. Since, as the apostle Paul writes, "we have this treasure in earthen vessels" (2 Cor. 4:7), the earthly part of us is not the most valuable aspect of personhood. Nonetheless, the church visitor should appreciate the sense of loss experienced, and should try to direct the patient's thoughts in a constructive direction.

Amputations may also signal changes in the patient's lifestyle and vocation. Depending upon the age, sex, and occupation of the amputee, the adjustment period will vary. Being fitted for and learning to use a prosthesis, an artificial limb or replacement, can be a stressful time, too. The church visitor's encouragement and support during this period are much needed. Adjustments to a possible vocational change may be difficult but mandatory. Again depression will be perhaps the dominant emotion. The church visitor should not minimize or discount these feelings, but should allow the patient to express them openly.

Other examples of subtractive surgery include procedures the results of which are externally visible, such as mastectomy, or breast removal. No less traumatic is a hysterectomy, or removal of the uterus, even though the results are not visible externally.

Both of these gynecological surgeries are subtractive and make the patient feel less feminine and womanly.

Corrective Surgery

In one sense all surgery is designed to correct some illness or injury. However, corrective surgery generally has no negative connotation. That is, it is perceived by the patient as beneficial and helpful. No sense of loss is involved. Examples of this kind of surgery are cataract removal and retinal detachment repair. These procedures relieve medical conditions and, it is hoped, result in increased visual acuity. Many orthopedic and cardiac surgeries (discussed more fully in chapters 12 and 16) can be included in this category also.

The church visitor might assume that since these procedures improve the patient's health and quality of life, there will be little or no anxiety. Such is not the case. Regardless of the anticipation of favorable results, few patients relish the prospect of surgery. Many patients fear the anesthesia and the sensation of "going under." Others have fear that the outcome will not be as satisfactory as hoped.

Another area which the church visitor should be aware of is that of pain control following surgery. Problems can develop from two directions. Some patients seem to need more pain medication than others. Individual thresholds for pain certainly do differ. Those who need a good deal of relief may actually come to depend upon the narcotic used and risk the possibility of addiction. Other patients fearing drug dependency may go to the other extreme and not request enough pain medication. Then the pain becomes so severe that regular dosages are not effective.

It may be that the church visitor can assist both types of patients by encouragement. The patient who desires more medication than is good for him may need support to stretch out the time between pain-relief shots. The other one may need encouragement to acknowledge that he needs medication for his pain, so that he does not attempt to be a "superman."

In a very small percentage of procedures complications may occur. Even a so-called routine surgery can go awry. For example, the patient may develop an infection. Such an unfortunate occurrence will lengthen the hospital stay. Understandably the church visitor may be needed to give extra support. Depression, which often follows a successful surgery, will be exacerbated in the case of complications.

Cosmetic Surgery

Cosmetic surgery is done to improve the patient's appearance. These procedures enhance emotional health as well as the physical quality of life. For example, a breast reconstruction following a mastectomy would come under this category. Many types of so-called plastic surgery are performed on persons who may have been involved in accidents causing facial injury. Certain congenital defects, such as webbed fingers and cleft palate and lip, are not life-threatening but require this kind of surgery.

The church visitor should appreciate the impact these surgeries can have on the well-being of the patient. Success of cosmetic surgery is as important to the patient as corrective surgery. Because of the emotions involved, confidentiality is especially important.

Other cosmetic surgeries, such as face-lifts and wrinkle removal, may be seen as improving the self-image of the patient. These procedures affect the patients' perception of themselves and are of significance and importance to them. Such needs may well be individually justified.

Exploratory Surgery

There may well be more anxiety attending exploratory surgery procedures than any other. Generally the patient has symptoms that cannot be explained by the usual battery of tests and diagnostic procedures. Uncertainty clouds the performing of exploratory surgery, and patients generally fear the worst. Biopsies are classic examples of this type of surgery. Tissue specimens are removed from an area or organ and sent to the laboratory for analysis. Sometimes the results may not be known for many hours.

Biopsies may be performed by injecting a needle into the area or organ in question. However, a laparotomy, an incision of the abdominal wall, may be necessary. This is more invasive and involves the insertion of a lighted probe into the abdomen and removal of tissue. Bronchoscopy is a procedure of looking down the throat into the bronchial tubes and lungs. An endoscopy permits the physician to look down the esophagus and take tissue specimens for laboratory examination. All these procedures are mildly painful and physically uncomfortable.

The church visitor can be of great help during these anxious times of waiting. Care should be taken not to give a blithe, offhand assurance that "everything will turn out okay." It may not. Share the concern of the patient and explore at his initiative possible outcomes and responses to those outcomes. The continuity of God's love and presence in all of life's events should be emphasized. If the patient gets a good report, the church visitor can rejoice with him. If not, the church visitor can be there for support and further ministry.

Emergency Surgery

Emergency surgery is distinctive not only in that time is of the essence but also in that it may be the result of trauma (sudden injury). An appendectomy is often an emergency procedure because of the possibility of rupture. Emergency surgeries are those which cannot be postponed or scheduled. They are not elective or anticipated. They are more traumatic than other surgeries because the patient has no time to prepare for them. At the same time the patient has little time to worry and has little or no responsibility for the decision to submit to surgery.

Emergency surgery is often associated with vehicular accidents. Internal injuries as well as broken limbs are often treated in the emergency room. Falls at home and industrial accidents may also require emergency surgery. The unexpected nature of this kind of surgery is anxiety-producing in itself. Emergency surgery also means that the patient and family may not have the surgeon or hospital of choice. This may add to the mounting anxiety. Also, the exact nature and extent of injury may not be known initially.

The church visitor can be of great assistance in such a time of crisis. It is greatly supportive for the patient or family to see a familiar face. Uncertainty can be much more manageable with such support. Prayer is an important part of this support. Invoking the healing power of God, the church visitor brings a steadying influence in a time of tremendous stress. Prayers should always be positive affirmations of God's care and presence. They should not attempt to limit God in such a way that unfavorable results make the patient or family feel that their faith was too weak.

The five categories of surgery presented here are not exhaustive and definitive. However, they provide the church visitor with a framework into which individual cases can be placed. A common theme throughout is the reality of presurgical anxiety and postoperative depression. These will attend most surgical procedures of any type. The church visitor's awareness of these reactions will enhance the effectiveness of his ministry.

Although the main focus of the chapter has been upon the patient, the church visitor may be of particular help to the family as well. Ideally, a visit to the patient before the patient is prepared for surgery is suggested. A corollary of this would be to sit with the family during the time of surgery. The oppressive atmosphere of the hospital waiting room is rarely conducive to relieving any anxiety. A sharing of the family's burden during this time of uncertainty is most beneficial to them, and will help them realize the caring presence of the church.

Follow-up visits after surgery are necessary also. Remembering to be sensitive to the patient because of his diminished physical energy, the church visitor can with the patient thank God for the success of the surgery. If the surgery has not accomplished all that the patient hoped for, the church visitor should share that disappointment as well. A follow-up visit is even more important to the patient when things have not gone well. Assurances of the church visitor's continued concern are vital. Such genuine caring can help the patient cope with whatever the future holds.

Finally, there is no such thing as minor surgery. All surgery is major to the patient. The church visitor should never assume that any procedure is so routine and risk-free that it can be ignored.

10

The Medical Patient

As has been noted, the distinction between a surgical and a medical patient is not rigid. Many medical patients become surgical patients, and surgical patients need medical care. However, there are several illnesses in which medicine alone is the treatment. Some of these are so minor as not to require hospitalization at all, such as the common cold and many allergies. Others are life-threatening and need the acute care provided in the hospital.

Three representative medical conditions, diabetes, asthma, and hypertension, may be controlled by home medication for the most part, but the church visitor will encounter these patients with some regularity in the hospital. These illnesses and the role of the church visitor will be described in the ensuing discussion.

Diabetes

Currently diabetes affects more than eleven million people in the United States (nearly five million of these are not aware of it). As is true of any abnormal physical condition, there are degrees of severity of this disease. For some the condition can be controlled by diet modification alone. Others require either oral or injected medication.

In most cases diabetes is a malfunction of the pancreas. The pancreas manufactures insulin to help the body cells absorb glucose, a type of sugar. If production of insulin is impaired by illness or injury to this organ, excess sugar remains in the blood, resulting in such diverse problems as retinal disease in the eye or poor circulation in the toes.

Because of the chronic nature of diabetes the church visitor is likely to encounter diabetic patients frequently. Patients can generally learn to handle their illness, although the more severe cases will require more adjustment. Age is another factor influencing the patient's ability to cope. Young people generally find it easier to give themselves injections than do older patients.

The church visitor should be sensitive to the dietary regimen and injection schedule of diabetic patients. Showing an understanding of patients' special needs is a way of expressing care and concern for them. The church visitor should be aware that each patient will react to this regimen differently. Most patients will handle these restrictions well, but a few may harbor continuing anger or denial.

Generally diabetes patients need injections only if their own insulin production is extremely low. Moderate cases often can be treated with drugs such as Orinase, which can be taken in pill form. One promising surgical treatment involves implantation of an "insulin pump," which releases insulin on a more regular and controlled basis than injections. Regardless of the treatment, it is very important that the patient follow the regimen established by the physician. When this regimen is not followed, blood sugar levels are "uncontrolled" and the risk of developing complications becomes greater.

In spite of precautions, diabetic patients may still occasionally require hospitalization. Many patients perform their own tests to determine the amount of insulin needed. If they misinterpret these tests and take an incorrect dosage, insulin shock may result from the lower sugar level in the blood. In such cases the patient may be hospitalized, even becoming comatose for periods up to several days. One can easily imagine the anxiety and fear of family members; thus visits in such times of crisis are especially important. Families should not have to go through such an experience alone.

Asthma

Asthma, like diabetes, is indiscriminate in that it affects persons of all ages and both sexes. It is the blockage of the airways

leading to the lungs. Due to allergy or other causes the membranes of the throat and bronchial tubes spasmodically contract
so that the flow of oxygen is impeded. When these spasms occur,
the patient becomes short of breath and may react with intense
coughing and "wheezing." The onset of an asthma attack is usually unpredictable, but it often can be controlled by medication at
home.

The asthma patient is hospitalized when attempts to restore
free breathing at home are unsuccessful. Severe asthmatic attacks
may need to be treated with more powerful medication given
intravenously. This is done in the hospital and the patient usually
stays for two or three days.

The asthma patient evinces several emotional reactions the
church visitor should understand. Perhaps the dominant feeling
is panic, which occurs when breathing becomes difficult. The
patient will describe his reaction with a statement like, "I didn't
think I was going to make it." When any normal reflex, such as
breathing, is interfered with, the person is apt to become very
distressed. Even though such episodes may not be long in duration, the asthma patient is very fearful that he may not get to the
hospital "in time."

The uncertainty about when a serious attack may occur leaves
the asthma patient with a lot of lingering anxiety. The patient
feels victimized and helpless to prevent another attack. This lack
of control and feeling of futility may also trigger a depressive
affect. The church visitor needs to give special assurances of
God's continuing love and care for these patients. Since they
become very tense when these episodes occur, their breathing
difficulty is compounded. The church visitor will aid the healing
process if he takes a relaxed approach and provides the patient
with biblical encouragement.

In addition to asthma, the church visitor may encounter
patients with a variety of pulmonary disorders that are also not
surgically correctable, such as emphysema and bronchiectasis. A
medical treatment of these diseases may not cure them, but it
will enable the patient to live better with them. Other illnesses
such as pneumonia and pleurisy are more acute and curable.

Hypertension

Hypertension (high blood pressure) is a vascular disease that
is generally treated nonsurgically. As with diabetes and asthma,

this condition is usually controlled by medication taken at home. Occasionally people will be hospitalized when their normal medication can no longer control their blood pressure.

Hypertension can develop in younger people, but usually it affects older patients. High blood pressure indicates the condition of the patient's blood vessels and as such is a symptom or indicator rather than a disease. It often signals an impending stroke or heart attack; therefore physicians seek to keep blood pressure within normal limits.

The church visitor should be aware that some instances of high blood pressure seem to be related to environmental stress, in which case hypertension may be temporary. It can be of great help to the patient to work through the causes of that stress. Stress reduction in a broad sense is the work of the church. Personal inner peace comes from the Lord Himself (John 14:27). It is hoped that the patient's faith will enable him to cope with this stress.

Most hypertension, however, is organic, and a medical regimen is needed to control it. Usually this is done with diuretics and drugs that enlarge the blood vessels. The church visitor should never presume that every medical condition has a spiritual origin. On the other hand, that possibility should never automatically be ruled out.

This chapter has touched on a class of patients that will be seen less frequently than others in the hospital setting. Medical patients generally have chronic illnesses that can only be treated, not cured permanently. The church visitor's role is one of support for patients who are variously restricted and limited. To give such support without encouraging self-pity is sometimes difficult. Ministry that fosters an unhealthy dependence on the church visitor is misguided. Allowing any patient to indulge in sympathy-seeking may well be a reflection of a patronizing attitude on the part of the church visitor. The distinction between giving needed encouragement and simply propping up a patient's emotions is sometimes fine indeed. In all instances divine wisdom is needed and is readily available (James 1:5).

PART THREE

Specific Patient Visitation

11

The Cancer Patient

As emphasized above, all illness involves spiritual as well as physical and emotional dimensions of the person. On this basic premise the ministry of the church visitor is built. The goals and purposes of this ministry are identical to those of the physician and nurse in that all seek to promote the healing of the whole person.

Healing entails the integration of that which was separated and the unifying of that which was fragmented. It is the opposite of dis-ease. The healing arts and pastoral care are dedicated to this concept of wholeness. In the New Testament salvation and wholeness were the work of the church and its Founder, Jesus Christ.

Perhaps no other disease is more fragmenting and disintegrating than cancer. There is a prevailing myth that cancer is always fatal and that death is always preceded by a lingering, deteriorating process. Actually many cancers can be permanently cured. Particularly if treatment is initiated quickly, a full recovery is the rule and not the exception. The church visitor may need to keep the patient from indulging in a fatalism that is neither spiritually nor medically justified.

The purpose of this chapter is to examine the special needs of the cancer patient and the role of the church visitor. In addressing this theme the emphasis will be on the therapeutic power of hope. This capacity of the human spirit will be explored as an adjunct to the medical and nursing care given. The apostle Paul writes that suffering produces endurance, endurance produces character, and character produces hope (Rom. 5:3–4).

Our discussion will be divided into three segments: the testing stage, the treatment stage, and the terminal stage. The role and approach of the church visitor in each of these stages will be dealt with. Although somewhat arbitrary and often overlapping, these stages seem to apply to many cases of cancer. A better understanding of these stages may help the church visitor relate to the cancer patient more effectively. Sometimes the cancer patient will be in the hospital; other times he will be at home and come to the hospital on an outpatient basis.

The Testing Stage

The cancer patient in the testing stage is usually in the hospital because of one or more of the danger signals. Public information and education by groups such as the American Cancer Society serve to alert persons to consult a physician at the onset of these symptoms. Generally patients manifest a mild degree of anxiety about the tests they take. This anxiety revolves around the testing procedure somewhat, but more specifically around the outcome.

During this diagnostic period the role of the church visitor is to support the patient and family through a time of uncertainty. Handling the unknown is difficult for most people. The visitor can often detect the patient's feeling of foreboding. Heightened anxiety is expressed by both tension and an almost manic level of conversation.

The church visitor will accept whatever mode of anxiety reduction is utilized by the patient, and will let the patient know it is all right to be scared. Hope should be offered to each patient. Hope is based on the patient's religious faith, which is directed toward God and grounded in His Word. It is more than positive thinking and contrived optimism. Hope is an anticipation and expectation of good, a belief that God is very present and a help. It is not a superstitious grasping at straws. It must not be polly-annish, but must acknowledge the gravity of the situation.

One cannot reassure patients by lightly dismissing their anxieties. In fact, the patient's level of anxiety can actually increase if his concerns are not taken seriously. If the visitor does not approach the matter with a proper amount of seriousness, his credibility and compassion may come into question. The visitor must also take care not to raise unrealistic expectations for the patient. He should discourage the patient from placing hope in treatments which have been proven not to be effective. The use of Laetrile, for example, may prevent the patient from receiving therapy that has been proven to be of help. At the same time the visitor can encourage use of other treatment modalities which are still mainly experimental, such as the laser beam, provided they are administered under proper supervision.

In the case of the cancer patient hope focuses on the outcome of the diagnostic tests. Legitimate hope is extended that the results of those tests will be favorable to the patient, specifically, that no malignancy will be found. If malignancy is diagnosed, there is the hope that it will be localized and in an early stage of development. That is, hope is offered for a good prognosis.

The church visitor must never present hope or encourage the patient in such a way that the patient feels any sense of personal failure or guilt if the primary hope is not realized. Care must be taken to assure the patient that the church visitor will share the disappointment of a hope unrealized. In other words, the church visitor should help facilitate a shifting of hopes if circumstances change. Visiting the cancer patient may mean helping him continually to change the focus of his hopes. If the hope in the diagnostic stage is not realized, then the church visitor must be prepared to offer support and caring presence in the next stage, the treatment stage.

The Treatment Stage

Cancer is basically a proliferation of cells. For reasons not completely understood the body's cell-building function goes awry. Almost any of the body's tissues can be affected. This means that cancer cells may develop in the major organs of the body, such as the lungs, liver, kidneys, or pancreas. These abnormal cells may also be found in the major structures of the body, such as the bones or blood. The location and type of cancer cells will give the oncologist (the physician who specializes in cancer treatment) an indication of what type of treatment is most appropriate.

Not all patients go through each stage or do so in the order presented. However, usually patients who are diagnosed as having cancer will undergo some form of treatment. Depending on the type and location of the cancer, three options (or a combination of options) are usually possible: surgery, chemotherapy, and radiation therapy.

For example, if a lung biopsy reveals malignancy, removal of the affected area or the entire lung, followed by radiation, may be required. The church visitor will seek to minister to the patient (and family) in all stages. When hope that the biopsy will be negative is denied, hope shifts to the successful treatment. This hope will be that the tumor is contained in but one lobe of the lung or that the malignancy affects only one lung.

These hopes are held by both the patient and family. Sometimes the family creates a "conspiracy of silence." They seek to protect one another from the bad news that cancer has been diagnosed. Often this indicates that they are unable to handle their emotions and to cope with the unpleasant reality. The church visitor may be able to assist in helping members of the family own their feelings and be as honest in their relationships as possible.

The church visitor may also be able to address the question most often raised by the patient and family: "Why me?" Too often patients have an unhealthy view of Deity, in which God is seen only as a vengeful, punishing force. Because of this, feelings of real and imagined guilt often surface and are expressed. The church visitor can be of great help at such a time by offering assurance of the love and forgiveness of God in a tactful and nonpatronizing manner. As a representative of God and the church, the visitor can help relieve some of these religious hang-ups.

Patients may demonstrate a certain amount of anger during this stage, partly because of their discomfort and partly from a feeling of being victimized. The church visitor can be of assistance in helping the patient direct this anger into constructive outlets. Sometimes this can be done by enlisting the patient and family in the "war" against cancer. If not properly redirected, anger often focuses on physicians, nurses, and family members.

Most importantly, the church visitor can be caring and present. To hope with the leukemia patient for a better blood count, to hope with the tumor patient that chemotherapy is reducing a growth, to hope for successful treatment and remission—all these are legitimate hopes. Helping the patient mobilize the healing power of his own body is part of any therapy. Supporting the patient through the side effects of chemotherapy and encouraging him to cooperate with the regimen prescribed make the church visitor's role a valuable part of the treatment program.

Sometimes, however, even with the best medical and spiritual care, patients do not respond favorably to any treatment modality. Then, unfortunately, the disease progresses beyond the point of reversibility. This ushers in the terminal stage.

The Terminal Stage

To be sure, there are many individual differences among cancer patients. Variables such as age, response to medication, other medical conditions, and time of discovery all come to bear on the patient's prognosis. With the right combination of variables, the patient can recover. Sometimes, however, even the best of efforts is not enough. The patient enters what might be called the terminal state: nothing seems able to stem the tide of the disease, and death becomes imminent. At this point the question of discontinuing the apparently unsuccessful treatment is raised. This issue involves not only the cancer patient but every patient whose illness is irreversible and who is maintained by life-support systems. In the case of the cancer patient the quality of life has to be one of the more important variables in making such an important decision. Thus when the patient's treatment, such as radiation, has an extremely adverse effect on the quality of life, such treatment may be discontinued even though it presumably extends the patient's life. The issue becomes a value judgment: is the patient's life or the patient's dying being extended?

Such an emotional and ethical question is not answered easily, and there are few generalizations that can be made. The church visitor obviously will never be a decision maker in this context, but support should be given to the cancer patient and the family when a decision has been made.

At such a time the church visitor's ministry becomes even more intensive. Hope is still offered to the patient; however, hope for cure and recovery shift into hope that pain can be controlled and that family relationships and business affairs will be in order when the patient dies. Most patients do not fear death as much as the potential suffering and indignity that may precede it. Too often cancer patients fear intractable pain, which is one of the prevailing myths about the disease.

The suffering of the cancer patient is not confined to physical pain. Often the deterioration of appearance and bodily functions are more dreaded. The church visitor is most effective at this point in assuring the patient of his worth and value as an individual. There is usually a marked depression in the patient at this time. Compounding this is the fact that sometimes the family becomes less supportive. Furthermore, because they wish to "remember him as he was," friends may not visit nearly as frequently.

All of this tends to make the patient discount himself even more. The church visitor should attempt to visit a patient in this stage more frequently, and affirm the patient's integrity as a child of God. At this point the patient may want to look beyond this life, and discuss or question the afterlife. Again hope of a better life and release from earthly pain and distress may be brought up by the patient.

In some instances the patient may use this period for confession or a review of his past life. Allowing the patient to air his feelings about the meaning of life may be one of the greatest helps at this time. Too often family and friends cannot handle this sort of conversation because they feel so close to the patient they are threatened. In an accepting and nonjudgmental manner, the church visitor will attempt to encourage such an evaluation on the part of the patient.

Perhaps as important as anything, the church visitor assures the patient that he will not be abandoned because of impending death. The fear of death is often a contagious malady, and if the patient senses that those about him are uncomfortable with death, he will react accordingly. The church visitor's role may be one of assuring the patient and family that love is stronger than death.

Ideally this stage of illness can bring the patient and family into a new appreciation for each other. At the same time there is the possibility that the prospect and event of the patient's death will place such stress on the family that permanent damage to the relationship among surviving members is sustained. This is particularly true of spouses at the death of a child.

Cancer patients, perhaps even more than other patients, need hope. The church visitor conveys hope to the patient in the testing stage that the diagnosis may be a benign illness. In the treatment stage there is the hope that the illness will be treatable and containable, and that the patient will make a full recovery. Hope in the terminal stage is for death with dignity and for a better life beyond this.

The possession of hope in time of illness and stress can be of significant help and benefit to the patient. The church visitor holds forth this spiritual quality to enable the patient to maximize his own therapeutic resources. The visitor approaches the patient with the same purpose as that of medical personnel and the care they provide—to speed the healing process.

12

The Orthopedic Patient

Orthopedic patients, those who have diseases or deformities of bones and joints, constitute a diverse population. They are represented by both sexes and every age group. Part of this is because they are hospitalized for both illness and injury. Generally those who are admitted because of bone and joint illness tend to be older, whereas victims of trauma (sudden physical injury) are often younger. This chapter will discuss distinctive facets of the orthopedic patient of which the church visitor should be aware. The discussion will be divided into three areas: a profile of the orthopedic patient, therapeutic procedures, and emotional and spiritual considerations.

A Profile of Orthopedic Patients

Unlike the cardiac patient, who is often a middle-aged male, the orthopedic-patient profile will be quite varied. However, on closer examination some refinement and generalization can be made. It is suggested that there are three classes of orthopedic problems which the church visitor may encounter: trauma-related, congenital, and degenerative.

Trauma-related Injury

Many orthopedic patients are hospitalized because of either vehicle accidents or injury received on the job, at school, or at home. Vehicle accidents most commonly involve cars and motorcycles; they may include airplanes, trains, and boats as well. Typically these result in broken limbs and damage to the rib cage and spine. These patients usually are admitted through the emergency room and spend some time in the intensive care unit before being transferred to the orthopedic unit. The extent of injuries will vary from minor to critical. Correspondingly the length of stay might be a matter of hours or months. Long-term patients need a lot of support from the church visitor to combat boredom and depression.

These patients will be of any age group and either sex. Motorcycle-accident victims are usually young males, but car accidents involve people of all ages. Trauma injury may involve both the accident victim and the one at fault. Occasionally others may have died in the accident. The church visitor should be aware of the range of feelings of all involved in traumatic injury. Care should be exercised not to be inquisitive about accident details, for litigation may be pending. The church visitor should not be perceived as taking sides or placing blame.

Other types of trauma injury, in addition to vehicular accidents, are those incurred at home, work, and school. Most orthopedic patients who are injured at home are the victims of some type of fall. Industrial injuries are caused not only by falls but also by heavy equipment, which has crushed some part of the body. Injuries sustained at schools often are the result of sports—sprains, breaks, and torn ligaments, for example. Again these trauma-related injuries, although they may involve people of all age groups, usually happen to younger, more active persons.

The church visitor needs to have a general knowledge of these kinds of injuries and the stress they produce. The worker may receive some kind of workmen's compensation, but others may be facing real financial hardship. Sports injuries may mean that the athlete will miss an important game or even the balance of the season. Knowing the possible ramifications of these kinds of injuries will enable the church visitor to empathize with the orthopedic patient.

Congenital Conditions

Orthopedic patients include those who need medical correction of congenital conditions. Some of these conditions, such as scoliosis, will affect preadolescents. Other conditions, such as clubfoot, are usually treated earlier. Most corrective procedures need to be initiated before the bone growth is complete. Younger patients may be in the pediatric unit instead of the orthopedic unit.

Fortunately advances in immunology have made polio virtually nonexistent. However, the church visitor will see older patients whose problems stem from a bout with polio in their younger years. Congenital bone and joint disorders literally can affect any bone or joint in the body.

Another disease that brings patients to the orthopedic unit is arthritis. Sometimes thought of as an older person's illness, it affects the young as well. Its causes are not completely understood, but this inflammatory disease causes many people a great deal of pain or incapacity. For some it may be a minor limitation, but for many arthritis is extremely debilitating. Rheumatoid arthritis is particularly damaging.

The church visitor will encounter patients who feel that arthritis is something of a curse, a punishment from God. Its appearance and progress do not seem to be related to lifestyle as do some other diseases such as lung cancer and cirrhosis. The mysterious onset and exacerbation of arthritis give rise to superstitious thinking in some. Helping the patient understand God's care in time of pain is a big task the church visitor faces.

Degenerative Conditions

In addition to accidents and congenital problems, other orthopedic patients are hospitalized because of degenerative conditions. Generally these occur in later life, but not exclusively. The complaint of a "bad back" is sometimes due to degenerative disc problems. The spinal nerves are irritated or damaged by the shifting of vertebrae; and instead of being cushioned by sufficient cartilage, the vertebrae become more vulnerable to further trauma and resulting pain. Injury can initiate this condition, but there is also deterioration caused by the aging process. The problem is often one of intractable pain.

Another degenerative condition the church visitor may encounter is osteoporosis. This is usually more pronounced in older women and is a result of hormonal changes which produce a calcium deficiency. Bones become softer and break much more easily than in earlier years. Many falls that result in broken hips may actually have been caused by the weakening and breaking of the bone just before the fall. In any event the bone is broken and the patient requires hospitalization.

An appreciation of these degenerative conditions may help the church visitor relate more empathically to these patients. Often there is a great deal of guilt and self-blame: patients may feel that they have brought the pain and discomfort upon themselves. Other complications may arise as well. Older persons who fall in their own home may live alone, and their family may feel that they are no longer able to function independently. Younger patients with disc disease may face the prospect of changing their vocation. All patients will need a lot of support and understanding from the church visitor. Showing care and concern in time of crisis is what being a church visitor is all about.

Therapeutic Procedures

Even cursory knowledge of the various treatments for the orthopedic patient will be helpful to the church visitor. To know something of these procedures will enhance the church visitor's credibility and enable him to converse more intelligently about the patient's condition and progress. This does not imply that the church visitor should make medical concerns the focus of the conversation, but neither can they be ignored. Showing some degree of comprehension of what the patient is undergoing will encourage the patient to talk more freely to the church visitor. The therapeutic procedures most often encountered are surgery, traction, and physical therapy; these may be used singly or in combination.

Surgery

Surgical intervention for orthopedic patients has become increasingly successful. The development and ongoing sophistication of joint replacements have made this the treatment of choice for many hip, knee, and ankle problems. For example, hip sockets that are virtually pain free can be made. By using a special cement, the head of a broken hipbone can be made stable. The hipbone is then fitted to a metal socket that gives strength to the hip's movement and eliminates any friction that might otherwise cause pain.

Another surgical technique involves using stainless-steel pins to hold a bone in place until it heals. These are removed when healing has taken place. In the same manner a metal rod may be placed parallel to a shattered bone to give the bone strength and stability, and it usually remains in place indefinitely. Procedures such as these may eliminate or minimize the need for heavy casts. If casts are required, many can be fabricated of an epoxy instead of plaster, as epoxy casts are both stronger and much lighter than the plaster ones. The larger the area needed to be in a cast, the more it is important to have a manageable cast. In some injuries a full body cast is required. Casts, like pins, not only allow bones to knit but also eliminate undesired movement.

In degenerative disc disease a testing procedure called a myelogram is often called for. This involves the insertion of dye into the spinal fluid. X rays then indicate if the normal movement of the spinal fluid is impaired and at what point. If surgery is required, a laminectomy, the surgical removal of a damaged disc, may be performed. Another surgery involves the fusion or joining together of vertebrae. This may limit movement somewhat, but will, it is hoped, relieve the pain of abrasive vertebrae movement. Usually surgery is considered advisable if other means of relieving pressure are ineffective.

Traction

Traction is used for several reasons. When a leg or arm bone is pinned, traction is employed to make sure there is no shortening of the injured bone while healing. Another use, in back or neck injuries, is to relieve pain and allow damaged vertebrae to heal without pressure. Traction is also used in cases of whiplash and lower back pain to avert the need for surgical intervention. The amount of weight used and the direction of pull are determined on an individual basis.

Being in traction can be a matter of a few hours every day to a constant regimen. The church visitor should be aware of the tediousness and restrictiveness of traction for the orthopedic patient. The church visitor's doing of small chores that might otherwise be painful or impossible for the patient is helpful. The church visitor should sit or stand so that the patient does not have to shift position in order to make eye contact.

Physical Therapy

Some type of physical therapy usually constitutes part of the rehabilitation of the orthopedic patient. Often this is begun shortly after surgery or may even be started upon admission to the hospital. Generally this involves exercising the affected muscles through such activities as weightlifting, stretching exercises, and practice in using a walker or crutches. Therapists are well trained and sensitive to patients' needs. They work with the attending physician and follow his regimen for the patient.

Physical therapy may be ordered for other than orthopedic patients (stroke patients, for example), but it usually is most useful for the orthopedic. In long-term programs the relationship between therapist and patient may become very strong. Sometimes that relationship provides the motivation an older patient may need to keep trying when progress is slow. Patients who live by themselves need to gain as much independence as possible before leaving the hospital. Practice in walking or climbing stairs may be skills necessary to regain after surgery.

Spiritual Support

The church visitor's role can be very instrumental in the recovery of orthopedic patients. Because the length of stay is often extended, a typical reaction of orthopedic patients is depression. They feel that progress is slow and irregular. Further, they may envision some temporary or permanent impairment. Financial strain may also be involved. All these things contribute to their depression; hence orthopedic patients need a great deal of encouragement and assurance of God's goodness. These assurances need to come from the church visitor's understanding of the problems that they face. Three sources of depression will be examined here.

Self-image

Orthopedic patients may perceive themselves differently because of a physical change. Amputation of an extremity produces a sense of loss. These feelings of loss are compounded by the importance the patient places on physical perfection. Younger patients generally, but not exclusively, are more conscious of this. Amputations, permanent braces, a limp—these things and many more may cause the patient to go through some type of grieving process, of which depression is a major part. To mourn sincerely with the patient is part of the support the church visitor can give. The church visitor may also be able to remind the patient that the dignity of being a child of God is not impaired by any physical, external loss or weakness. According the patient such integrity can be a major factor in the recovery process.

Pain

The very nature of orthopedic problems dictates that some degree of pain will be present. Having to tolerate constant pain, the orthopedic patient is prone to depression. Chronic pain is depressing; ironically, many types of pain medication leave the patient depressed also. Another complicating factor is the patient's fear that the use of pain medications may become addictive. Going without sufficient medication means that the pain may compound so that substantially more pain medication is necessary to alleviate it. These larger doses may actually contribute to the dependency the patient is trying to avoid.

The church visitor may find the patient depressed about this vicious circle. Encouraging responsible and reasonable use of pain medication may be helpful in this regard. Sometimes diversion can safely stretch the time between pain medication. Engaging in conversation or perhaps a game can help the patient become weaned from taking medication excessively. Caring for the patient as a person may also obviate the patient's indulgence in self-pity.

Dependence

A third contributor to depression is the loss of capacity, that is, of certain abilities, which makes the orthopedic patient dependent upon others. Whether the incapacity is temporary or permanent, the feelings of helplessness and vulnerability are profound. Incapacity is no respecter of age, for it can happen to anyone; and of course at no point does one relish relinquishing responsibility. Some patients attempt to use their dependency to manipulate others; that represents a desire to exercise a certain amount of responsibility.

The church visitor can help the orthopedic patient by avoiding an overly sympathetic, patronizing attitude. Any help offered and given should be done simply and matter of factly. A good approach is to help the orthopedic patient realize that not only are all people dependent upon God, they are all dependent on each other as well. Recovery can be hastened by generally involving the orthopedic patient in some problem or interest beyond himself.

13

The Geriatric Patient

Demographic studies indicate that the average age of the population is continually rising. This means that there is an ever-increasing number of aged persons in our society. There are a number of myths and stereotypes that often distort society's view of the aged. One of these myths is that most of the aged are senile and need to be cared for in institutions. Actually most senior citizens are living in their own homes. Another myth is that senility is an inevitable part of the aging process. A third is that the aged are grouchy, difficult to relate to, and living only in the past.

The church visitor needs to be aware of these prevailing stereotypes because the aged, as a group, are often neglected due to these myths. It becomes very apparent that there are huge differences in the effects the aging process has on an individual. In a very real sense aging begins at birth and continues thereafter. Studies indicate that the aging process is, in part, hereditary. That is, heredity seems to dictate which parts of the body wear out first.

Chronological age, the number of years a person has lived, is not necessarily the same as biological age, the measure of one's physical condition, although they tend to be parallel. A sixty-year-old man may have a body that appears to be only forty. Since women live longer than men, the aging process also differs according to one's sex. It is becoming more apparent that mental acumen does not decline dramatically with aging. Physical conditions such as arteriosclerosis or vitamin deficiency seem to be more a factor in senility than age.

Because aging does produce a slowing down of the body's resistance to trauma and disease, the church visitor will encounter a substantial number of elderly people with some degree of deteriorating physical health. This chapter will focus on the geriatric patient in three contexts: at home, in the hospital, and at the nursing home. This will be followed by a discussion of suggested ways of relating to the geriatric patient wherever met.

Home

Geriatric patients may be seen by the church visitor in their own home or the home of a relative, for most physical problems keep them close to home but do not require any kind of institutionalization. Their spiritual needs are no less real, however. Because of the infirmity of age they may not be able to attend church services regularly, if at all. Too often the congregation forgets about them. A planned program of visitation to homes of the elderly is a very fine way to keep in touch with them and assess their needs.

More and more churches are providing such things as wheelchair ramps and hearing aids in pews. These will be of great help to those who are marginally homebound. The church visitor may wish to set up a network by which the aged are called daily on the telephone. Though not a substitute for a personal home visit, it can be a valuable complement to a regular itinerary.

Generally the church visitor should attempt to schedule home visits on a regular basis, for older people tend to be more comfortable with a "routine." It might seem that the homebound would have so much time at their disposal that this would not be necessary. However, it is the norm for the homebound to feel less energetic. This means it takes them longer to complete routine tasks of personal grooming and light housekeeping chores. Usually a nap is also a part of their agenda. So it is a courtesy for the church visitor to call ahead and plan a visitation schedule with them that is mutually satisfactory.

Hospital

The nature of the illness or injury of the hospitalized geriatric patient will dictate the role of the church visitor. As with patients of any age, the basic principles of hospital courtesy apply. However, there are certain distinctive aspects of relating to the geriatric. Keeping the following suggestions in mind may help the church visitor enhance his ministry to geriatric patients.

1. Respect the geriatric patient's dignity and integrity. This means that the church visitor will view the geriatric patient as a child of God. His worth and basic value is not diminished in spite of the physical deterioration that often accompanies aging. The geriatric patient is more susceptible to disease and injury and will usually have to be hospitalized more often and for longer periods than people in other age groups. For this reason the church visitor will often have more opportunity to relate to the aged in the hospital than to other age groups. Because of their value, hospital visits should be as frequent and long as possible.

2. Respect the opinions of the geriatric. The church visitor must never assume that senility automatically comes with age. Many geriatric patients' mental faculties are superior to others younger than they. Geriatrics may appear to be less flexible in responding to new ideas and concepts than others. Many indeed do feel that they have "heard it all." Closed-minded thinking is not necessarily the product of age, however. Too often the ideas of geriatrics are not taken seriously. This is unfair to both geriatric patients and the church visitor. Their wealth of experience entitles the aged to an audience. Their ideas concerning their needs may seem to be idiosyncratic, but they represent their own feelings about themselves. The church visitor should not lightly dismiss their complaints, if any, about hospital care, but should perceive them with the same concern as he would those of a patient of any age.

3. Listen to the geriatric. There are two ways the church visitor can carefully listen. On one hand he should take seriously the information geriatric patients convey to the church visitor about, for example, their needs. A second way is to allow them the opportunity to communicate. A good hospital visit requires that the patient not be "tuned out." Obviously not all geriatric patients are founts of great wisdom, but neither are all so incoherent that their words should be ignored.

Creative listening is almost a lost art. To listen with an empathy that is able to draw out the deep concerns of the spirit is the goal of the church visitor. This ability to listen springs from a genuine concern and love for the geriatric patient. Listening with "the third ear" enables the church visitor to ask meaningful questions and make perceptive observations. To listen carefully is to gain the trust of the geriatric patient.

Too often the elderly have low esteem and feelings of little worth. Unfortunately our society tends to equate the value of a person with his productivity. However, the church visitor can reinforce the sense of worth of the geriatric patient by the love reflected in careful listening. Listening also means taking seriously the expressed concerns of the geriatric patient. The church visitor may be able to perform small favors, such as bringing the patient's mail from home. Other things the visitor does, such as looking after a pet or arranging for transportation home from the hospital, may express the love of God in a very tangible way.

4. Do not rush the geriatric patient. We live in a fast-moving world. Changes occur with great rapidity. At times the geriatric patient in the hospital feels that same rushed pace. The elderly usually are physically slower and do not respond as quickly as younger patients. The church visitor should be alert to this and pace the conversation accordingly. Long pauses do not necessarily mean that the geriatric patient is not interested in conversing; this may simply mean that time is needed to organize thoughts and catch one's breath. Brusqueness is not appropriate; patience is.

The church visitor should attempt to create an unhurried and calm atmosphere in the visit. Small chores performed for the patient may be appreciated also. A walk with the patient, for example (with the nurses' consent), should be done at the patient's own rate. Keeping the patient's needs foremost is part of communicating respect for the geriatric.

Sometimes the geriatric patient feels rushed to make decisions. Again the church visitor can be of assistance by helping him to sort out those things which are indeed urgent matters from those which are not. For instance, the patient may need an intermediate level of care following an acute illness or trauma before returning home. This decision will be made by the patient, family, discharge planner, and the institutions involved. The patient may feel lost in the shuffle and need not only assurance about his future, but frequent explanations of the process. The church visitor can do this, taking time to repeat whenever necessary. Care should be taken not to have the patient feel pushed or pressured. This helps keep the patient's integrity intact.

5. Try to understand the geriatric patient. The church visitor should attempt to enter the perceptual world of the elderly in order to minister to the geriatric patient. This means a sharing of his fears and concerns as well as his hopes and aspirations. The elderly often face similar fears: fear of falling and breaking a limb with no one around able to help them; fear of crime—of being attacked in or out of their home, or of being robbed; fear of financial insecurity; and fear of being an imposition on family or friends. These fears are not restricted to the elderly, but age exacerbates these concerns. In the hospital setting some of these fears, such as finances, may be heightened; while others, such as falling, are lessened. Many of these same concerns extend to the geriatric patients who are residents in nursing homes.

Nursing Home

The church visitor ministering to the geriatric in the nursing home finds a variety of needs there. Because of the long-term aspect of patient care, such institutions differ from the acute-care hospital. For example, the ratio of nurses to patients is considerably less. This means that the type of geriatric patient cared for will be in less need of constant nursing care. Within nursing homes the level of care may be designated as either intermediate or skilled.

Whatever the type of care offered, it is generally more custodial than curing, and residents usually remain at the nursing home until death. For many families the nursing-home option is not first choice. Unfavorable stereotypes and the desire of the elderly to be independent make many residents reluctant to be admitted. Families often bear a sense of guilt in this process. Though unable to care for a member adequately at home, the family is hesitant to place him at the nursing home.

The church visitor can understand that with these dynamics operating, ministry is certainly needed. Too often the geriatric patient in a nursing home feels rejected, abandoned, and unhappy. Residents who have been independent may have some adjustment problems. To give support and reassurance to the resident is an important task of the church visitor.

Geriatric patients, in any environment, want to be independent and not patronized. They need to have family contact and support. They need to communicate and feel needed and appreciated.

In a very real sense their needs are no different from any other age group.

The church visitor can be of great help and support to geriatric patients. Some of their needs are unique to their time of life; other needs are common to all society. Whether homebound, hospital-ized, or in a nursing home, geriatric patients need to have regular contact with the church visitor. By being attentive to their need for small favors, the church visitor can personify God's loving care for the aged.

Again it should be emphasized that in spite of myths about the elderly, most are able to live independently, can manage their own financial resources, and are alert mentally. Like patients at any age, geriatric patients thrive on the love and concern of others. To respect the integrity of the aged—sick or well—is a biblical concept: "You shall rise up before the hoary head, and honor the face of an old man, and you shall fear your God; I am the LORD" (Lev. 19:32).

14

The Pediatric Patient

An area of hospital visitation that should not be neglected is the pediatric unit, even though the church visitor may feel somewhat uncomfortable in relating to young children and adolescents. Some of this anxiety may be due to a type of identification. That is, the church visitor may have a child or grandchild who is the same age as the patient he is visiting. The realization that "this could be my child (or grandchild)" may inhibit the church visitor. This discomfort may be compounded because the adult perceives the sick child as more helpless than a sick adult. Furthermore, if the child is terminally ill, the visitor will feel that the child has not had the opportunity to experience much of life.

Yet another difficulty in counseling with children and adolescents is the problem of communication. The church visitor may feel a sense of hesitancy because conversation may seem stilted. Adolescents, and particularly young children, are not just small adults. They often possess an embarrassing frankness and directness that is hard to handle. Also, adolescents may perceive an adult as a person who does not or cannot understand them. The church visitor as a perceived authority figure has to indicate a genuine openness to the child's and adolescent's world. He must be able to enter that world comfortably to establish rapport and credibility with them.

This discussion will deal with three general age divisions: (1) infants and toddlers (0–4; generally, critically ill babies will be in the neonatal intensive care unit, while very young children will

93

be found in the pediatric unit); (2) young children (5-12); and
(3) teen-agers (13-19). These divisions are arbitrary and are not
meant to imply that any development or maturation occurs
when they are crossed. Rather, they are intended to provide only
a framework for a general examination of each age group.

Infants and Toddlers (0-4)

Characteristically the infant or toddler's parents are the focal
point of the church visitor's ministry. Their presence in the hospital room may well be an invitation to minister. The direction and
tone of the conversation will be largely influenced by three factors: (1) the physical condition of the child; (2) the emotional
stability of the parents; and (3) the family's experience with
hospitalization. The greatest anxiety will be encountered when
(1) the child is critically ill; (2) the parents are emotionally
unstable; or (3) the child or parents have had either a negative
experience or none at all with hospitalization. Any combination
of these variables may be present. It is necessary to ascertain
these factors early in the visit for an effective encounter.

Physical Condition

Children of this age can become critically ill in a matter of
hours. Accidents, of course, can happen immediately. Because
there is so little time to reflect on the infant or toddler's condition, parents are usually in a state of shock. The suddenness is
often overwhelming and hard to handle.

The church visitor may have difficulty fully appreciating the
anxiety of parents in this situation. Ministry at this point is caring
presence. It may be helpful to make some remark like, "Little ones
can surely get sick quickly," or, "I imagine this came about rather
suddenly." Permitting the parents to recount the events leading
to the child's hospitalization may help to discharge some of the
emotional tension and facilitate acknowledgment of the reality.

Emotional Stability

People react to the stress of a child's illness in a variety of ways.
Because the onset of a major illness often is mistaken for a minor
illness, the conscientious parent may react to this error with guilt.
Sometimes the illness may seem to be or actually is the product
of parental neglect or direct abuse. Because of societal norms, the

parent who abuses a child will display either remorse or defensive denial. Both emotions may be indulged in to a pathological degree. In other words, the emotional health of the parents before the child became ill will be reflected in their response to the present stress.

Generally parents will react to real or imagined guilt by overprotection. They will insist on being with the child at all times and doing things for the child. Possibly they will interfere with routine nursing care and treatment plans. In this way they try to make up for real or imagined deficiencies in their care of the child.

The other extreme is the parents' projection of anger at the staff. Parents who feel helpless or victimized by their child's illness generally will be extremely critical of the physician and nurses. Their anger may be overt or disguised; they may blame themselves, each other, or the other children for the child's illness or accident. Often, however, this anger is projected onto the staff and the church visitor. Fathers particularly may intellectualize on their child's illness by becoming overinterested in the disease itself, or in the drugs or machinery in use.

Experience with Hospitalization

If a child's prior hospitalization was successful and reasonably pleasant, the anxiety of the parents will probably be lower than if there has been no experience with hospitalization or an unpleasant previous hospitalization. In either event the trauma of hospitalization is shared by the family. Whatever is stressful for the child will be stressful for the parents. Hospitals are becoming increasingly aware of this fact.

As the church visitor becomes aware of the interaction of the physical condition of the infant, the emotional health of the parents, and the family's experience with hospitalization, the chances for a meaningful ministry are enhanced.

Young Children (5-12)

Not only are there tremendous individual differences among children of the same age group, there are great developmental differences between children of various ages. Obviously the span between a five- and twelve-year-old is great. However, some generalizations can be made about elementary-school children. They are not as dependent on their parents as are infants and toddlers, but they are not as independent as teen-agers. They are prepubescent, yet they are very conscious of peer as well as family expectations.

This means that the church visitor will relate to the child on a one-to-one basis. This does not preclude a ministry to parents, but adds a dimension not present in relating to infants and toddlers. In visiting with children in this age bracket two feelings must be dealt with: the emotional and spiritual impact of separation from family, particularly siblings, and ignorance and fear of hospital routine and procedures.

Separation

Boys particularly will disguise their sense of loss at being separated from the family. A boy's fear of being considered a "sissy" may reinforce his reluctance to show his feelings about such separation. He may wish to impress female nurses with his manliness and mask his anxiety at being away from home for perhaps the first time. Girls may have less desire to create such an impression, but they feel the same anxiety.

Such anxiety about separation and hospitalization may even be reinforced by certain restrictions on visiting. Because young children are generally prohibited from visiting in the hospital, both siblings and peers will visit seldom if at all. Although the loneliness and feelings of abandonment are partly offset by the nursing care and attention, nonetheless a visit from the church visitor may be quite welcome. Relating to younger children may be enhanced by bringing them some gift like a small toy or coloring book. Using hand puppets to tell a story (or let the child make up a story) may be helpful in identifying areas of special concern to the child. For older children, reading material will be a thoughtful gift.

Fear

Because hospitalization is a unique experience for most children, a certain amount of fear is usually evident. There is a certain difficulty in explaining to a child in understandable terms the meaning and purpose of routine medical procedures. Because of the kind of care some children receive when they are sick at home, hospitalization may be a difficult experience. These children are made to feel guilty, to feel it is their own fault when they become ill, although their behavior is usually not related to the illness at all. Such children may feel that they are an imposition and inconvenience to the nurse. On the other hand, some children are pampered and showered with attention and favors at home. They may be demanding and very self-centered.

In any event children are likely to feel some fear in their novel situation. The church visitor may be of help in allaying such fear by letting the child know it is all right to be afraid. Often the antithesis of fear is knowledge. By supplying bits of general information at the appropriate time the church visitor may help overcome those fears. However, the visitor should not give technical explanations; sometimes adults forget that a child's level of comprehension is still limited even with proper explanation. Full explanations and information should be communicated to parents.

The church visitor can help the child to communicate with his parents and the hospital staff. In addition, the church visitor can provide assurances of God's care and providence by caring presence and genuine concern. We specially emphasize *genuine*—children have the uncanny ability to see through much adult sham.

Teen-agers (13–19)

Teens are a challenge to minister to under the best of circumstances. When as a result of illness or accident they are hospitalized, ministry may be even more difficult. Two characteristics seem to emerge in adolescence: emotional shifts, and concern about self-image. There are no doubt many more, but these two seem more pronounced during the stress of hospitalization.

Emotional Shifts

The transition from the dependence of childhood to the independence of adulthood is not smooth. Neither is it predictable. In the hospital the same teen may exhibit very adult behavior at one time and very childish behavior at another. These variations in behavior reflect rapid changes in attitude.

Much of the frustration the church visitor experiences in relating to teens is rooted in this phenomenon. In one encounter the teen may want to talk in an adult manner on adult themes. The next contact may be characterized by childish folly. It is important that the church visitor recognize this shift as normal. It is not necessarily an invalidation of the teen-ager's identity. One must accept the child in the teen, for even adults have childlike traits.

The church visitor should be aware that teens are continually experimenting with varieties of behavior to see what affect these might have on adults. At the same time rapid shift in a teen's behavior may be a clue to some underlying stress that should be addressed. A direct approach may be helpful in discovering the source of this stress. For example, the church visitor may say, "You seem a lot quieter than the last time we visited. Is something bothering you?" It is important that the church visitor discern these mood changes without judging them as wrong or bad.

Teens are not necessarily uncooperative simply because they are teens. Teens on drug regimens (such as steroid medication) tend to be less compliant. The main variable seems to be how effective the drug is perceived to be by the teen. If a teen believes the medication is helpful, he will take the dosages recommended, whereas the teen who does not feel his regimen is effective will tend to resist.

Self-image

Problems of a poor self-image are characteristic of adolescence. Low self-esteem, low self-worth, and depression are all too common. Unfortunately self-destructive behavior may result from these negative feelings. The church visitor should be aware of this disturbing reality. To increase a teen's sense of self-worth and value as a child of God is an important contribution to the teen's mental health. The church visitor may need to reinforce the image of God as loving and accepting, particularly in teens whose family is less than that.

In a culture that deifies success and accomplishment, even a healthy teen may feel inadequate and unworthy. To help a teen accept himself as a unique creation of the Almighty is a difficult process. It certainly cannot be done by one person in one place at one time. However, the church visitor can contribute to the process. This kind of facilitation is an important task regardless of the teen's physical problem. The insecurity bred by illness or accident makes it even more demanding. To assist a teen on the road to maturity is a rare opportunity and the result is well worth the effort.

15

The Renal Patient

The medical treatment of end-stage renal, or kidney, disease has been radically transformed with the advent of hemodialysis. The "kidney machine," a great breakthrough barely two decades old, has been responsible for maintaining patients who would otherwise be terminal. So successful was the treatment that in 1972 legislators passed Public Law 92-03, by which Medicare coverage was extended to patients with end-stage renal disease.

Whether renal disease is caused by ischemic disorder, glomerulonephritis, or organ damage, the new technology gives hope where previously there was none. The technique involves diverting blood from the body through the kidney machine, allowing cellophane membranes in the machine to filter impurities from the blood, which the kidneys are no longer able to do.

Technology has improved, of course, and dialysis machines have become increasingly sophisticated. Generally most patients are dialyzed two or three times a week for three or four hours at a time. In 1974, 15,749 patients underwent maintenance dialysis, according to Social Security statistics; it is estimated that by 1984 that figure will be 55,360.

These figures give the church visitor some indication of the scope of renal disease. Initially it might seem that these patients, whose lives are thus extended, would have few, if any, emotional problems. Such is not the case. In fact the renal dialysis unit in most hospitals is a place where the church visitor may make a most significant contribution.

In order to develop an appreciation of these problems, it is necessary to review the various modes of treatment for or medical management of renal disease. We will discuss five options currently available to the end-stage renal patient: (1) hospital hemodialysis, (2) home hemodialysis, (3) peritoneal dialysis, (4) transplantation, and (5) cessation of treatment. We will also make some suggestions about how the church visitor may conduct his ministry to each of these patients.

Hospital Hemodialysis

As indicated above, in this country hemodialysis is potentially available to all patients with chronic renal disease. Patients are treated as near their homes as possible, and only in remote rural regions is distance a major problem. If it is, patients can usually arrange to visit a medical center or hospital when necessary. This requires a good deal of mobility for many dialysis patients.

Basically, hemodialysis is the filtering of nitrogenous waste from the blood. For some the process is relatively painless and amounts to little more than an inconvenience. For others— unfortunately the majority—dialysis is quite an ordeal. Frequently unpleasant symptoms such as leg cramps, sudden drop in blood pressure, itching, and nausea occur.

In addition to these organic reactions there are external discomforts as well. The insertion and extrication of the needle is painful. A certain amount of body exposure is necessary if the graft is in the upper leg, which may be emotionally painful. Even if the shunt is in the arm the patient may perceive it as cosmetically offensive. For some individuals these subjective factors are very painful indeed.

Although there is not a great deal that the church visitor can do to alleviate physical discomfort, he may certainly have an impact on the patient's emotional distress. In fact, the caring presence may even alleviate that portion of physical stress that is aggravated by fear and anxiety. It is important for the church visitor to be aware of the reality of the patient's pain and to develop empathy for that suffering.

Another aspect of hospital dialysis the church visitor should note is the social climate of the renal dialysis unit. It is inevitable

71250

that each patient becomes acquainted with fellow patients. On the positive side a spirit of camaraderie will develop, which can be very supportive. The negative facet of this is that when a fellow patient develops a complication, it may tend to demoralize the entire unit. A clotted shunt or cardiac arrest can significantly raise the anxiety level of the rest of the group. The church visitor again needs to be aware of this kind of impact and to be sensitive to changes in the patient brought about by events in the unit.

Home Hemodialysis

The main difference between hospital and home dialysis is that neither the strength or weakness of group dialysis affects the home patient. Even though home dialysis is somewhat less expensive than hospital dialysis, most patients opt for hospital care. Probably the most significant variable is the relationship with the person who is responsible for the treatments, often the patient's spouse.

Another advantage of home dialysis is the lessened risk of infection because only one patient uses the machine. However, the chore of keeping the machine clean usually falls to the spouse also. Added to this is the responsibility of injecting the needle—causing necessary pain to someone emotionally close. These are, no doubt, further reasons that most patients choose hospital dialysis.

The church visitor's role is basically one of support. A number of patients who initially attempt home dialysis change to hospital dialysis, a transition that often results in stress and tension (as does the transition from hospital to home dialysis). The church visitor's understanding reassurance can relieve patients (and their spouses) who change modalities from being saddled with a sense of failure.

Peritoneal Dialysis

A relatively new treatment in the management of renal failure is continuous ambulatory peritoneal dialysis (CAPD). This procedure differs from hemodialysis in that the removal of uric waste is not done by the filtering of the blood. Instead a tube or catheter is surgically implanted into the patient's peritoneal cavity. A container (usually a strong plastic bag) is attached to the outer end of the inserted tube. The bag is filled with a saline solution which flows through the catheter into the peritoneum by gravity flow. Then the procedure is reversed in about four hours. The saline solution, which now contains uric waste, is drained back into the bag, which is then emptied and refilled with fresh solution.

The advantages of CAPD are obvious. The continuous process of purging means that blood pressure fluctuations are not nearly as marked as in hemodialysis, and that symptoms caused by the rapid lowering of blood pressure are alleviated. Also, the patient has a great deal more mobility. The only limiting feature of CAPD is that one must exchange fluid and keep the opening around the tube sterile. New bags are used each time and are relatively inexpensive.

The main disadvantage of CAPD is that self-care has to be very cautiously monitored since the danger of infection, mainly peritonitis, is always present. This restricts its application to responsible adult patients. Furthermore, for some patients the CAPD is difficult to regulate in that too much fluid may be lost. Hemodialysis is more amenable to monitoring. However, these disadvantages may be reduced with further development and research.

The role of the church visitor for renal patients choosing CAPD is somewhat different from that for the hospital-dialyzed patients. Since the danger of infection is imminent, the shift back to the kidney machine may be necessary. To help the patient cope with the usual disappointment that accompanies that change is one function the visitor may have. Often there are a degree of self-blame and a sense of failure that need to be addressed as well.

Transplantation

A fourth approach to kidney failure is to remove the nonfunctioning organs and transplant a functioning kidney from a living donor or cadaver. The surgical removal of diseased kidneys is relatively uncomplicated, but it may be impossible with certain types of disease, for example, glomerulonephritis.

While transplantation would seem to be a panacea for end-stage renal disease, it poses several serious problems. One major problem is the lack of suitable kidneys for transplantation. Also, because of the body's immunological system, rejection of the donated organ is a possibility. Drugs that are used to minimize rejection, such as prednisone, have potentially dangerous side effects.

Ideally the donated kidney comes from a close family member. Compatibility is checked by blood cross-matching, but even then the possibility of rejection still exists. The chance of rejection is even greater when the transplanted kidney is from a cadaver.

The surgical implantation of the donated kidney is complicated. The kidney is placed in the abdomen and connected to the blood and urinary systems. The patient is monitored carefully following surgery, which lasts about six to eight hours. Expected hospital stay is about two weeks.

The need for spiritual support during this process is obvious. In addition to the anxiety that precedes any major surgery, there is also the added stress of uncertainty of outcome. Success rates vary, but no medical centers have yet achieved notable success. The church visitor can assist both the recipient and the donor by encouraging honest expression of their fears and hopes.

In the unfortunate event that a kidney transplant is unsuccessful, ministry to the recipient and donor involves giving comfort in time of double loss. The donor has lost a functioning organ, and the subtractive surgery is irreversible. Further, the expected satisfaction of improving the quality of life for a loved one is denied. This is to say nothing of the recipient, who has had high hopes dashed, and has undergone a good deal of suffering only to experience futility. The recipient may already feel guilty or selfish in having accepted the healthy kidney from a loved one. If it is rejected, these feelings of guilt may well be exacerbated.

All in all the replacement of a kidney is extremely stressful even if the surgery is successful. Possibly there may be resentment, even anger, on the part of the donor because of the attention focused on the recipient, especially if they are siblings. After the surgery the donor may have second thoughts and be fearful that his remaining kidney may not function properly. To be available to all involved in these traumatic times is risky, but rewarding.

Cessation of Treatment

The last option is not a treatment but the conscious decision to stop any further treatment. Some patients find physical and emotional adjustment to any form of treatment almost impossible. Others have had one or more transplant failures and feel the future holds no hope for them. Still others have so many medical complications as to preclude any reasonable hope of attaining an acceptable quality of life. These kinds of renal patients may opt to discontinue treatment.

The moral issues involved here are difficult at best. Variables such as age of the patient, extent of permanent damage to other body systems, and home and family relationships all come into play. Also involved are the expressed wishes of patients and their ability to make a meaningful choice.

As in any other dimension of human behavior there are great individual differences in the ability to cope. Coping with the limitations and restrictions to lifestyle that accompany kidney failure is never easy or simple. Particularly as the duration of treatment lengthens, patients ponder whether the effort is worth continuing. It is hoped that each patient is able to verbalize these feelings in an atmosphere of understanding and acceptance. The church visitor can help by actively listening to patients who are indeed questioning the meaning of life itself.

Giving support during this time should not involve giving advice, even if asked. It does mean that the church visitor can affirm any decision of the patient and family, whatever direction they choose. To discontinue treatment is tantamount to succumbing to terminal illness. Death occurs in about a week. Pain is controllable and coma generally precedes expiration. To be with the patient and family and affirm the dignity of life is always an indispensable part of the church visitor's role.

It is likely that few renal patients will choose this course of action. The church visitor will more frequently encounter patients who tend to disregard the limitations of the disease. They will take in excessive amounts of liquids and foods that are high in potassium. This results in larger weight gains than desirable and means longer and possibly more uncomfortable dialysis treatments. This behavior is a mixture of denial and anger and is similar to the emphysema patient who persists in smoking and the diabetic who eats sugar. It may not necessarily be a subconscious death wish as much as an unwillingness to accept the reality and seriousness of their illness.

These, then, are five ways a patient may respond to end-stage renal disease, and also some ways that the church visitor may be of service. Being available as a friend and part of the patient's support system is to demonstrate the love of God in a very concrete way.

16

The Cardiac Patient

Like cancer, heart disease has a negative emotional as well as physical connotation. Perhaps because of the high mortality and disability rates of the past, the cardiac patient experiences a profound sense of loss. Fortunately recent medical advances have made heart disease much less a threat to life than before. Full recovery from the effects of heart disease is not unusual. The church visitor can justifiably convey encouragement to the heart patient. To be sure, heart disease can and does cripple or kill. In most cases, however, if adequate treatment is begun with the onset of the symptoms, a full recovery is not unrealistic.

Though other major organs are no less indispensable, the heart assumes a greater significance. Part of this may be because it has been thought to perform other than physical functions. In both the Old and New Testaments (e.g., Ps. 19:14; Heb. 4:12) the heart is used to denote one's innermost being. David saw the heart as needing cleansing from sin (Ps. 51:10), and Jesus taught that sin comes from the heart (Matt. 12:34). In contemporary society it is the seat of emotions, for we love someone "with all our heart"; indeed, we are commanded to love the Lord in this manner (Deut. 6:5).

As with many other diseases, heart trouble is the product of both internal and external factors. There appear to be hereditary factors over which the patient has no control. But there are aspects of one's lifestyle (e.g., smoking, exercise, diet) that the patient can control. The church visitor should support cardiac patients in making any adjustments in their lifestyle that will enhance their recovery.

The church visitor will encounter the cardiac patient receiving treatment in the hospital and recuperating at home. In the hospital many heart patients will be in a special cardiac care unit, while others will be in a unit where less intensive medical and nursing care is needed. Visiting in the cardiac care unit is often restricted to the immediate family, but nurses can convey greetings and expressions of concern to the patient. On other units visiting is permitted, but the church visitor should keep it as brief as possible since the patient's energy level is low.

In this chapter the various types of heart disease and their treatment will be examined. Implications for the church visitor will be discussed as well.

Heart Disease

The church visitor should be aware that there are many different types of heart disease, each having a different treatment and prognosis. The type of illness will affect the type of ministry and visiting needed. Four main types of heart disease will be touched upon: occlusive disease, rheumatic disease, arteriosclerosis, and congestive disease.

Occlusive Disease

Occlusive disease may be the most common type of heart disease. Technically it is a disease of the arteries that supply blood to the heart. These coronary arteries become occluded or blocked by a build-up of plaque within the artery walls. The gradual narrowing of these blood vessels reduces the flow of blood to the heart. If the artery becomes completely blocked, the area of the heart muscle affected can be irreparably damaged. This lessening or shutoff of blood may cause chest pain (angina) and even pain in the jaw, neck, shoulder, and arm. When the heart muscle is deprived of blood and the oxygen the blood carries, the patient experiences what is known as a "heart attack," or myocardial infarction.

Attacks vary in severity, symptoms, and prognosis. Unfortunately for some a massive infarction is fatal. Others experience great heaviness in the chest and abdomen and become short of breath. Still others experience an attack so mild as to be unnoticed or mistaken for some other illness. The amount of damage done dictates the appropriate treatment modality, generally medication or surgery.

In addition to the coronary arteries, the blood vessels leading to the head are sometimes affected by this build-up of plaque. This condition, marked by dizziness and blackouts due to diminishing blood flow, is referred to as carotid stenosis. Another type of occlusive disease is the blockage of the main (femoral) arteries flowing to the legs. This limiting of blood to the lower extremities produces leg cramps and cold feet.

In all cases the occlusion of arteries is the cause of illness. Build-up of plaque seems to be related to cholesterol and high-density lipo-protein levels in the blood. There also appears to be a difference in the rate of plaque development between men and women of the same age, suggesting a hormone involvement. Lifestyle (smoking, lack of exercise, stress) also plays a part in how fast plaque is deposited. However, the church visitor should bear in mind that studies are not completely conclusive. No assumptions should be made about contributing factors in any individual case.

Rheumatic Disease

Another form of heart disease is linked to the bacteria that are associated with rheumatic fever. This infectious disease, usually affecting children and adolescents, may cause permanent damage to the heart valves. In later life the patient may experience weakness upon exertion. This is because these damaged valves impair the pumping capacity of the heart; that is, the heart chambers do not close properly and all the blood is not emptied. This back-up prevents efficient distribution of blood to the rest of the body. Whereas men in midlife are more prone to myocardial infarction, generally women are affected by rheumatic disease. Untreated, it can likewise be crippling or fatal.

Arteriosclerosis

This form of blood-vessel or vascular disease involves not only the blocking of the arteries but the hardening as well. It is generally associated with aging. Blood supply is limited as arteries lose their flexibility.

Often the arteries in the brain are hardened, and high blood pressure may create blood clots in them, causing them to burst.

This produces bleeding in the brain (cerebral hemorrhage) or stroke. Depending on the size of the burst artery and the area of the brain it serves, symptoms may involve loss of motor function (paralysis) and higher cortical functions (e.g., speech and memory). Severe ruptures can result in death.

Congestive Disease

Like arteriosclerosis, congestive heart disease is generally associated with the aging process. In this disease the heart muscle weakens and cannot pump fast enough. Fluids then build up in the lungs, producing a condition called pulmonary edema, and place greater pressure on the already weakened heart.

Another type of heart disease that might also be mentioned is congenital heart disease, marked by anomalies and birth defects. For example, the wall between two chambers of the heart may not be completely closed. The "hole" in the heart is generally detected early and treated surgically. Fortunately these conditions are not very common.

Treatment

Having some idea of the different types of heart disease will enable the church visitor to understand the treatments that are administered to the cardiac patient. These treatments will often involve a period of assessment in the hospital.

Occlusive Disease

Typically after a heart attack the cardiac patient may be hospitalized for a period of time, during which the heart muscle is allowed to heal itself. Then some period of time after his release the patient is brought back to the hospital for tests. These tests will enable the physician to determine the severity of the patient's occlusive disease.

For this purpose a cardiac catheterization is performed. This surgical procedure takes one to two hours and consists of having a slender, hollow rubber tube (catheter) inserted in a vein or an artery of the patient's arm or groin. The catheter is fed into the heart chamber and a dye is injected through it into the heart. The progress of the dye is monitored as it proceeds through the coronary arteries. Severely blocked arteries will allow very little of the dye to pass through, thus indicating a high degree of blockage.

This is a delicate procedure and involves some risk. The information derived, however, is extremely important and justifies the process. Depending upon the number of arteries affected and the percentage of blockage, the cardiologist will prescribe either medicine that expands the arteries and allows more blood through or surgery to by-pass the affected vessels.

By-pass surgery, or revascularization, is the taking of an unoccluded blood vessel (usually a vein in the leg) and grafting it into the coronary artery system so that the heart will receive the desired flow of blood. This surgery is generally very successful and is one of the more common surgeries performed, although there is risk (as with all surgery). Surgery on the carotid and femoral arteries may involve "reaming out" the affected vessels or by-passing them.

Rheumatic Disease

Catheterization is done for rheumatic disease patients as well. Leaky valves can be detected and the severity of that leakage assessed by this test. Again surgery may be required. Valve surgery involves either the repair or the replacement of the diseased valve. Replacements may be synthetic (teflon, for example) or animal (usually a pig's valve). Surgical intervention is very successful with the rheumatic disease patient also.

Arteriosclerosis

Surgery is less an option in this disease, since the overall condition of the blood vessels does not allow grafting. Patients afflicted with this often are given medicine to increase the flexibility of the vessels along with drugs to reduce high blood pressure. In case of a stroke, treatment may require speech therapy, physical therapy, and perhaps some type of occupational therapy. Treatment will, of course, depend upon the area affected and severity of the damage.

Congestive Disease

Treatment is mostly medical, although heart transplant may well become more of an option. Factors that must be considered are the age and general health of the patient as well as availability of a donor organ. Diuretics to increase the kidneys' discharge of body fluids are usually prescribed. If the disease affects the rate of heartbeat as well, implantation of a pacemaker may be required. Again the treatment of choice will depend on individual variables.

Implications for the Church Visitor

For the church visitor cardiac patients present a variety of spiritual needs. The needs vary not only from individual to individual, but among the types of heart disease as well.

Occlusive Disease

Sudden death is more a threat with occlusive disease than with the other types of heart disease. For this reason fear of death is very real to the patient who has had a moderate to severe heart attack. The typical patient is male and middle-aged (forty-five to fifty-five). Family responsibilities may be at their peak because of children in college. Realization of one's vulnerability and the unpredictable nature of most heart attacks are unnerving. The church visitor should be open to the fears of the patient. Sometimes it seems to help to have the patient verbalize the experience he has just come through.

In addition to very real fears, the cardiac patient will often exhibit a good deal of anxiety. Some physicians suggest that high stress and anxiety predispose a person to occlusive disease. That such anxiety would carry over when the person becomes a patient is understandable. The church visitor should be aware of this factor and let the patient express his anxieties. The church visitor may gently help the patient sort out those anxieties that can be addressed by concrete actions from those that cannot, and should generally demonstrate his willingness to help. At the same time the church visitor should realize that some anxiety may be as much a symptom of as a reaction to heart disease.

A certain amount of guilt may be felt by the patient who feels, rightly or wrongly, that his lifestyle is responsible for his disease. The church visitor may wish to explore this avenue, not in the stance of a confessor, but as an understanding friend. By being uncritical the church visitor may create a climate in which the patient can ventilate his feeling. Discreet use of Scripture describing forgiveness and new beginnings may be appropriate.

Rheumatic Disease

It is possible that the rheumatic disease patient may be angry that he did not receive proper treatment as a child or that the disease was contracted at all. Such feelings are usually expressed by the phrase "Why me?" Valve disease may not be detected until later in life, when family responsibilities are greater. If the patient is the sole breadwinner of the family, financial anxiety will be present. If the patient is unmarried, he may feel some guilt that his surgery is a drain on his parents' finances. As with any major surgery, there is fear of failure and of death. The church visitor should be aware of these feelings and give appropriate assurances of God's unfailing good purpose for the patients. He should focus on the enablement that such surgery will gradually allow.

Arteriosclerosis

Often it is difficult to communicate with patients who have had a stroke. Generally they will be elderly. If speech is affected it is difficult to use conversation as a means of therapy. Many stroke patients also weep inappropriately when spoken to. This lack of emotional control is embarrassing to the patient, but should not hinder the church visitor from engaging the patient in continued conversation. Allow time for the patient to regain composure and continue the visit. If the patient becomes too confused and disoriented, it may be helpful for the church visitor to give the spouse and family extra support. Even the confused and disoriented patient needs presence and a kind touch.

Congestive Disease

Like patients with arteriosclerosis, most of these patients will be in the older age group. The church visitor will have to be especially sensitive to their needs. For example, he may want to be there if pacemaker surgery is performed. Unfortunately the prognosis of this illness is generally unfavorable. To be with the patient in time of discouragement is extremely important. The church visitor becomes, in a way, the personification of God. To be there and care is the proof of God's love.

This chapter has discussed four diseases of the heart (and vessels). These four generally affect different segments of the population. Treatment for these separate diseases differs also. The church visitor's approach should take into account these differences when relating to the cardiac patient. A general knowledge of the type of illness and its treatment is the foundation upon which caring communication is built. Implicit in such an approach is emphasis on the patient as a person—not as a "case." While he should be as well equipped and prepared as possible, the church visitor also needs to beware of any tendency toward impersonalization. Seeing each patient as a unique creation of God and loved by Him will ensure a vital and concerned relationship. This is important when visiting cardiac patients, for many of them experience almost overwhelming anxiety.

Appendix A
A Glossary
of Common Medical Terms

Body Parts

aden   gland (adenoid)
arthr   joint (arthritis)
cardi   heart (cardiogram)
cephal   head (cephalometer)
cost   rib (intercostal)
cyst   bladder (cystitis)
derm   skin (dermatologist)
encephal   brain (encephalitis)
gastr   stomach (gastroscope)
hem(at)   blood (hemoglobin, hematin)
hepat   liver (hepatitis)
lip   fat (lipoprotein)
lith   stone (lithotrity)
my   muscle (myalgia)
nephr   kidney (glomerulonephritis)
ophthalm   eye (ophthalmologist)
oste   bone (osteomyelitis)
ot   ear (otology)
pulmon   lung (pulmonary)
rhin   nose (rhinoscopy)
thorac   chest (thoracic)

113

Procedures

centesis   puncture (amniocentesis)
ectomy   excision (mastectomy)
opsy   examination (biopsy)
plasty   plastic surgery (rhinoplasty)
stomy   new opening (colostomy)
tomy   incision (lobotomy)

Other Common Terms

a (or *an*)   without, not (anorexia)
algia   pain (neuralgia)
brachy   short (brachycephalic)
dys   bad, abnormal, faulty, difficult (dyspepsia)
hyper   more, above (hyperactive)
hypo   less, below (hypothermia)
itis   inflammation (laryngitis)
lys   breaking down (lysin)
megal   enlarged (megalocephaly)
osis   abnormal condition (neurosis)
path   disease (pathology)
penia   deficiency (leukopenia)
scler   hard (arteriosclerosis)
tachy   fast (tachycardia)

Appendix B
Suggested Scripture Readings and Prayers

Scripture Readings

Encouragement

Joshua 1:9
2 Chronicles 16:9
Psalms 27, 46, 57, 62
Isaiah 40:28-31
Romans 8:28-30
Ephesians 3:14-21

Comfort

Psalms 23, 121, 131, 139
Matthew 6:25-33; 11:28-30
John 14:1-6, 27
1 Corinthians 15:51-58
2 Corinthians 1:3-7

Hope

Psalms 42, 63, 84, 90
Isaiah 55:12-13
Romans 5:1-5; 8:35-39
2 Corinthians 5:1-5

Thanksgiving

1 Chronicles 16:8-34
Psalms 30, 36, 65, 92, 100
Ephesians 5:18-20
Philippians 4:4-6
1 Thessalonians 5:16-18

Prayers

Before surgery:

Heavenly Father, we thank You for Your love and healing grace. We bring before You __(patient's name)__ and ask that You give him/her a special sense of Your presence here in the hospital. Guide the surgeon's hands and use his skill so that this operation may speed the healing process. Bless the nurses and all who have a part in this procedure. Grant __(patient's name)__ a quick recovery; may he/she draw upon Your strength in the days of recuperation ahead. We ask these things in Jesus' name. Amen.

When diagnosis is undecided:

Lord, we thank You for __(patient's name)__ and for his/her trust in You. Be with him/her and help him/her to feel Your love and healing presence. Give the doctors, nurses, and technicians special skill and wisdom as they conduct and interpret these various tests. May the information they derive help __(patient's name)__ to get well and return to his/her home soon. Give __(patient's name)__ special grace in this time of stress and uncertainty. These things we pray with thanksgiving in Christ's name. Amen.

When recovery is uncertain:

Our loving Father, we thank You for the reality of Your continual presence with us. We praise You for Your promise that You will never fail or forsake us. In this time of need we pray on behalf of __(patient's name)__ and ask that You lay Your healing hand upon him/her and raise him/her to health and wholeness soon. Give the doctors and nurses special wisdom and discernment as they help __(patient's name)__. Enable him/her to respond favorably to the medicine, care, and treatment he/she receives. Ease any pain and discomfort he/she might have, and keep him/her close to You. Bless his/her family while he/she is here in the hospital. Watch over and protect our dear brother/sister. In Jesus' name we ask this. Amen.

When tests and treatment are favorable:

Dear God, we rejoice in Your goodness and thank You for (patient's name) fine recovery. We praise You for helping him/her to get along so well here at the hospital. Continue to give him/her assurance of Your love and healing grace. We thank You for the doctor's skill, the nurses' care, and for all who had a part in the healing process. Restore   (patient's name)   to complete health and wholeness soon. Grant him/her the gift of patience and help him/her to experience that peace which comes from relying upon You. Again we thank You and acknowledge that all healing comes from You. Keep us ever mindful of Your grace and goodness. We ask this in the name of Jesus. Amen.

When recovery is not likely:

Heavenly Father, our hearts are heavy and we need a special measure of Your grace. In this hour of difficulty we come to ask You for Your strength and guidance. We ask that Your perfect will be accomplished in the life of   (patient's name)   . In our selfishness we would pray for his/her recovery, but most of all we ask that Your good purpose for him/her be accomplished. We cannot understand Your ways fully and we find it hard to accept what we cannot understand. Give us grace in this time of trial as well as strength and courage beyond our own. Be with   (patient's name)   and all his/her family and loved ones. Keep them close to You and to each other. We ask this in Christ's name. Amen.

Appendix C
Case Studies

Visit before surgery*

The patient is a fifty-three-year-old woman who will have surgery the next morning. Church visitor knocks, is invited in, and sits on a chair next to the patient's bed.

Church Visitor: Hello, Mrs. Doe, I'm _____ from _____ Church. I've seen you at church recently and am sorry to see you here at the hospital.

Patient: Hi, _____ . Yes, I'm sorry to have to be here, but glad to get this taken care of. I'm scheduled for surgery first thing in the morning.

CV: Surgery always sounds kind of scary to me.

 P: I guess I am getting more apprehensive the closer it comes. It's not that I don't have confidence in the doctor or anything like that. . . .

CV: I'm sure it's very normal to feel that way. Most of the people I visit before surgery feel the same way.

 P: Sometimes I think if I had more faith or was a better Christian I wouldn't worry at all.

*A similar approach may be used for patients awaiting administration of medical regimen or therapy.

CV: Faith is something we can all use more of. Having faith doesn't mean that we won't be concerned about ourselves. We should be. It does mean that we trust and depend on God to enable us to keep those concerns in their proper place.

P: I never thought of it that way. I just felt guilty for worrying.

CV: It's not wrong to experience an honest emotion. Jesus wept when He felt sorrow, so we shouldn't be ashamed of our feelings either.

P: I just hope everything goes okay.

CV: Let me assure you that all of us at church are thinking of you and praying for that very same thing. May I share some Scripture with you and then pray?

P: Yes, please do.

CV: (Reads and prays.) Some of us from church will stop and check on you in a day or so when you get to feeling better. I believe the pastor will try to stop by in the morning. Good night, Mrs. Doe.

P: Good night, _____ . Thanks so much for coming.

Visit after surgery: favorable results

The church visitor returns to see Mrs. Doe two days after her surgery.

Church Visitor: Good afternoon, Mrs. Doe. I just wanted to stop by to see how you're getting along after your surgery.

Patient: Thanks for coming. I'm doing fine. Still a little sore and uncomfortable, though.

CV: I hope that it eases and that you feel better every day.

P: I'm sure glad to have it over. Everything went well; the doctor is very pleased with the way I'm recovering. He calls me his "star patient."

CV: Well, I'm certainly happy to hear that. I knew it would be a big relief.

P: Yes, I feel that a big load has been lifted. As you know, I wasn't particularly looking forward to having surgery. But I'm thankful it's done.

CV: All of us at church share your joy.

P: I really appreciate the prayers and concern of everyone. It helped.

CV: I agree. I believe God answers all our prayers in His way and time. I know you're still not feeling your best, so may I offer a brief prayer of thanks?

P: Please.

CV: (Prays.) I'll run along for now, and one of us will be checking on you in another day or so. Glad you're making such fine progress.

P: Goodbye, and thanks for all your help.

Visit after surgery: unfavorable results

The church visitor returns to see Mrs. Doe two days after her surgery.

Church Visitor: Good afternoon, Mrs. Doe. I wanted to stop by to see how you're getting along after your surgery.

Patient: Thanks for coming. (Begins to weep.) The doctor didn't have very good news for me.

CV: What did he say?

P: He said that the surgery would not help as much as he had hoped. I might even have a permanent disability.

CV: I'm so sorry to hear that.

P: . . . and I prayed so hard.

CV: It's hard to understand why our prayers were not answered the way we wanted.

P: God must be punishing me. I know I haven't been a very good Christian.

CV: Mrs. Doe, none of us are what you call a "good Christian." We all have a lot more learning and maturing to do. I don't know why things aren't going the way we all want for you. It takes a lot of faith to believe God loves us when our most earnest prayer seems to be denied.

P: That's right. I guess I didn't have enough faith.

CV: Maybe it's more a matter of the direction of one's faith than the amount of one's faith.

P: What do you mean?

CV: I'm not sure, but I believe God's love surrounds us even in the bad times of our life and gives us the strength we need to carry on.

P: I think I understand. You mean that it takes as much faith to cope with disappointment as it does to get what our first choice would be.

CV: You said it much better than I could. I'd like to pray that God will continue to show you His love even in a time of loss and discouragement.

P: Please do. I need it.

CV: (Prays.) All of us at church continue to be concerned about you and will be here for you whatever direction your illness takes.

P: Thanks for coming. It means so much to know you all care.

p 89,90
94-forpaper— 71250